# PEDALING
# ACROSS AMERICA

Happy Travels.

Lolly

*How 3 Oregonians*
*carried 153 years and 702 pounds*
*across the Continental Divide*
*and the Great Plains*
*against headwinds, 18-wheelers and fatigue*
*—fueled by pancakes and*
*the kindness of some friendly folks—*
*and made it over the Appalachians*
*4146 miles,*
*all the way to Virginia Beach,*
*in 56 days*
*—with only 12 flat tires*

# PEDALING ACROSS AMERICA

by
DON and LOLLY SKILLMAN

VITESSE PRESS • BRATTLEBORO, VERMONT

DEDICATED TO THE PEOPLE
WHO DARE TO DREAM—
AND FOLLOW THROUGH

*Maps by Robert MacLean, copyright © 1988 by FPL Corporation*

*Design by Irving Perkins Associates.*

*ISBN 0-941950-21-2*
*Library of Congress catalog card number 88-050963*

*Published by Vitesse Press*
*A division of FPL Corporation*
*P. O. Box 1886*
*Brattleboro, VT 05301*

*Manufactured in the United States of America.*

# CONTENTS

*Contents*

A photo section follows page 90.

*May 21*

# 1

# *TWO STEPS BACK?*

WEST YELLOWSTONE, MONTANA—DRUMMOND, IDAHO

It had not been a day notable for luck, and from the looks of things that wasn't going to change now. Judging by their dress, the two at the bar were working men. Suspenders held up their heavy trousers and one had on a sheepskin coat, leather side out, that had seen a lot of use. Both men were giving me unfriendly, almost belligerent looks.

The bartender must have been worried about the electric bill, because the lights were low in the dingy room and he didn't smile. All three stared at me, especially at the bright yellow rainsuit and rubberized shoe covers I was wearing, and at the bicycle helmet in my hand. Apparently nothing about the way I looked pleased them.

Water ran off the rainsuit, dripping onto the worn pine floor, floating little particles of oiled sawdust up out of the cracks. This was not, apparently, the first time the floor had been spilled upon. The odor of stale beer and cigarette smoke thickened the air, and through the gloom I could make out, against the side wall, the curved glass front and ornate, colored plastic decoration of a big, old-fashioned record player. The wind roared outside, almost shaking the building, driving sleet and snow horizontally.

If you are wondering what bicyclists were doing out in this kind of weather, so was I. It was a bad situation, and I was just beginning to realize it. And because I hadn't wanted to stop earlier in the day where there was food and shelter, it was my fault. But we hadn't anticipated that the mountain passes in Yellowstone Park would still be clogged by winter snow in late May. In order to get back on our coast-to-coast route as quickly as possible we were forced to detour around the park to the west. We were behind our schedule.

# Riding Day *18*
## *69* ROUTE MILES

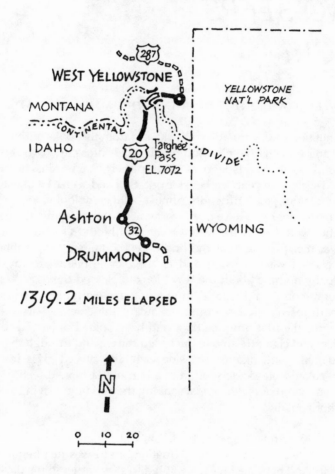

That very morning in West Yellowstone, after learning our route was blocked, my brother Bill, my wife Lolly and I had carefully checked our maps. Reluctantly, we decided that the best detour was west, *back* into Idaho, which we had left a week before, and then southeast to rejoin our planned route. As we folded and re-packed the map, resigned to a change that would add 100 miles to our ride, we noticed the weather for the first time. Dark, leaden clouds hovering halfway up the mountains were already dropping a few snow pellets to make sure we knew who was boss. It promised to be a lousy day. As we pedaled out of West Yellowstone, a steady headwind served notice that the ride around the park was not going to be easy.

Tall lodgepole forests lined both sides of the road with thin, spindly trunks scarcely an arm's length apart, supporting a dense canopy overhead. The wind blew hard against us as we rode along, three strange creatures whose pumping legs never touched the ground, yet whose white-helmeted heads bobbed with effort. Dressed in yellow rainsuits to protect against the wind, we looked like space-ready astronauts. We noticed the chill when the wind increased, and the temperature fell as we climbed away from the valley over a mountain pass. The exertion of the climb was welcome because it kept us warm.

Gradually, the country we rode through became depressing. Where-just a few years before had been a beautiful lodgepole forest, dead or dying trees now stretched for miles in every direction. Thousands upon thousands of acres of trees had been destroyed by pine beetles. Only a few live clumps remained, and here and there, as if on futile guard duty—either very hardy or perhaps untasty—a single mature tree. Ordinarily, the tiny green seedling trees, which might someday replace the forest and offer hope for the future, would have made me feel good, but today the hope wasn't strong enough to overcome my gloom.

We passed a few roadside homes, many of log construction, that looked invitingly solid. No one was outdoors, and it was easy to imagine warm, crackling fires inside. We passed a large Forest Service complex and it, too, looked deserted.

Around noon, we reached a spot where the highway paralleled the Henrys Fork of the Snake River for a few miles, and here tourist facilities had sprung up, mostly catering to fishermen. One cafe in particular, made of rustic peeled logs painted a dark, Smokey Bear brown, looked inviting. It was warm inside, where walls and booths were of varnished knotty pine. A couple were the only other customers, and they stared at us, confirming the unusual sight we made in our cocoon-like clothing. We took off our rain gear and sat down at a booth. Instantly we felt chilled through.

The man from the kitchen wore a white apron and carried his order pad with practiced confidence.

"Hi," he said, smiling, "I'm your waiter today. I'm the cook too, and the owner."

"Hi," Bill replied. "A little cold out there."

"Where are you from?"

"We're from Oregon," Lolly said. "We're headed for the east coast."

"How about that?" The owner was enthusiastic, probably because we had already proven ourselves just by being here, over 1,000 miles from the Oregon coast. The couple overheard, and they soon lost their shyness. We found ourselves talking about our trip as we ate. Gradually the hot food dispelled our chills; it was pleasant sitting there enclosed by the thick log walls, getting warm and looking out the windows past our bikes leaning against the building to where we could see the river flowing westward. But we couldn't stay in the booth forever. We finished, paid the owner, said good-bye to the couple, and elbowed back into our rainsuits. Almost reluctantly we went back out into the cold and climbed on the bikes.

Early in the afternoon the sun found a few ragged holes in the clouds, which immediately closed ranks as if it had been a mistake to allow us even a short burst of warmth. The overcast dropped lower, like a gray, undulating ceiling, and we found ourselves riding through the previews of an impending snowstorm. At the bottom of a long hill near the river we passed a parked state police car, and Bill went back to ask about road conditions and the weather.

"He thought we took the best detour around the park," Bill reported. "He said the weather shouldn't get any worse."

His forecast was encouraging. We turned south at the little agricultural town of Ashton, across the railroad tracks and past the farm co-op building before heading out into the country again. There were a couple of small motels in town, but we didn't usually stop this early, and I was anxious to cover as much ground as we could.

Turning south had an immediate effect. With the 25-mile-an-hour wind at our backs we sailed along, our rain gear bulging out in front of us like balloons. It was thrilling, being propelled with such ease, after grinding against the wind since early morning. We didn't even mind the sleet that began to accompany the wind because our helmets and clothing protected us from behind. Effortlessly we pedaled farther and farther away from Ashton, through rolling country where fields of grain stretch to the sky and ranches are far apart. Then, when we were far enough from the motels to make returning against the wind impossible, the road turned ninety degrees and settled down for some serious, long-distance, country crossing.

As soon as we rounded the curve the gusty crosswind blew us half-way across the road before we could correct balance and direction. Stinging particles blasted our faces. After several miles of sleet rasping at our faces and blurring our vision, we knew we had to find shelter. But the wide grain fields provided no protection, only a waving, bowing acquiescence to the wind. We hadn't seen a ranch for a long time and the storm-blurred horizon ahead appeared empty.

A few miles farther as we topped a slight rise, the sight of a cluster of unpainted buildings gave us a feeling of relief. They were snuggled into a hollow, as if taking dubious shelter from the terrain.

"That must be Drummond," I muttered, remembering the name on our maps. But the tiny settlement looked deserted. A huge grain eleva-tor loomed through the storm, the upper portions fading into and out of sight in the scudding clouds like a ghost. The whole place looked unreal in the blowing storm, but a light glimmered from inside the nearest building on the corner.

And so we found ourselves inside the bar, facing the three men.

"Where can three bicycle riders pitch a tent out of the wind?" I addressed the bartender, hoping the gray in my hair would lend some credibility and offset our strange garb—maybe even elicit some pity.

"Nowhere I know of, not out here." The bartender's tone was flat and noncommittal, and the other two just stared. Unlike the helpfulness of most people we had met, the attitude of this trio was not hospitable.

There was silence for a minute or two as we looked at one another. Finally, one of the men at the bar observed that the wind would be weaker down in the canyon by the creek. "Just go down the side road until you come to the creek. Plenty of room to camp."

It slowly dawned on me that we were being turned out. Whether we felt it was adequate or not, we had just received all the help we were going to get.

Back outside, when we discussed camping down by the creek, Lolly looked unhappy and Bill wasn't showing much enthusiasm either. We pushed our bikes around a sheltering corner of the building to talk it over, and came face-to-face with a huge Doberman. Luckily the dog was tied by an oversized chain, the farthest reach of which was marked by a worn semicircle in the dirt and mud a scant yard from our feet; lunging and slobbering, he began to bark frenziedly.

We quickly decided that Drummond was an unfriendly place to be, and started down the side road, teetering to keep our balance in the wind. The dog's barking faded as the road promised pavement, became gravel and then, having lured us, turned into a devilish clay. We wavered down into a small canyon where the wind and sleet, if anything, were concentrated by the terrain.

The creek was muddy and swift; newly leafed willows on the banks flogged one another viciously in the icy gusts. There was no place to camp out of the storm. We considered returning to the bar, or braving the Doberman in hopes of finding someone at home. Now if only someone were actually living in that abandoned farmstead over there by the creek . . . .

Abandoned?! We glanced at each other for a second, and then took off for the place with amazing alacrity. With a newly found disregard for private property, we quickly parked the bikes in the lee of one of the sheds. The door came open easily after we pried off a nailed crossbar. There was room, but just barely, for the tents in between the more serious leaks in the roof. At least we're out of the wind, I thought, and we can replace the crossbar when we leave. So what if the roof dripped on the tent?

Soon the little gasoline stove was roaring, and we were warming our hands on cups of steaming chocolate. Even the freeze-dried dinner tasted extra good, testimony to the 70 hard miles we had ridden that day. As it grew dark, the sleet turned to snow and the leaks dripping onto our tents stopped. We were eighteen days into our ride across America. With over 3,000 miles still to go, this camp in Drummond represented a new low in accommodations. What, I wondered, will we run into next?

*Spring 1985–May 3, 1986*

# 2

# WHY?
# THE BEGINNING

How had we come to find ourselves in such a god-forsaken place? Adventure is okay, even exciting. But when you're over fifty, and you're cold and you hurt, and a survival-aware portion of your subconscious keeps rehearsing hypothermia treatments, you begin to wonder: what am I doing here?

The idea to ride across America was spawned on a completely different kind of day, warm and sunny. In 1985, Lolly, Bill and I took a bike ride down the Oregon coast. We were comfortable in bright jerseys and riding shorts, getting tanner by the hour as we enjoyed the blue ocean, whitecaps and waves. Sandy beaches beckoned us, high cliffs added their stature, and every now and then sand dunes stretched away into the edges of dense coastal forest. A dependable tailwind pushed us southward at an unhurried pace. The restaurants and campgrounds were good and we were having fun.

"Wouldn't it be fun to ride all the way across?" Lolly asked near the end of the trip.

"Across? Across where?" I fell for it.

"Across America."

My brother and I exchanged glances. I knew my wife was just supposing, and Bill knew she was just supposing.

Beware of idle talk, because once you say the words, they have a way of working on you. Insidious little nudges will come into your conscious thoughts, spinning pleasant scenarios of adventure to come. Anticipation centers on scenes set in warm, comfortable environments where dangers are welcome because of the excitement. Before we knew it, we were talking about actually riding our bicycles across America. An opposing thought kept occurring to me—why? Why ride that far?

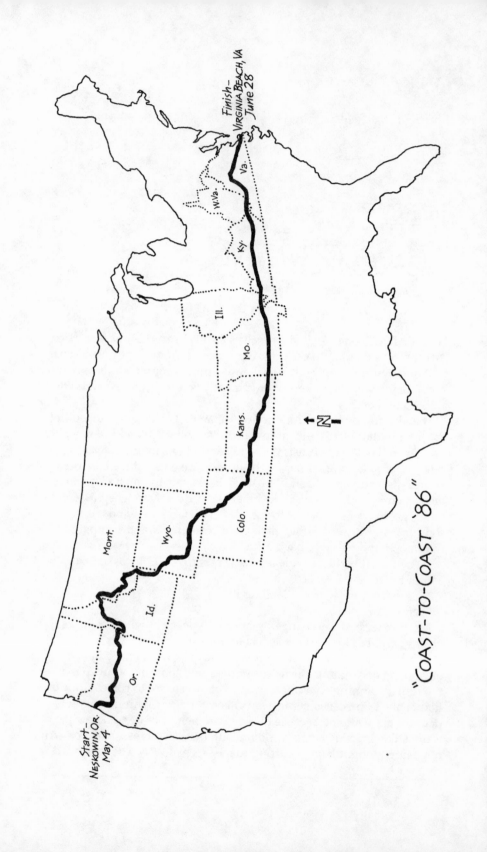

Start –
NESKOWIN, OR.
May 4

Or.

Id.

Wyo.

Mont.

Colo.

Kans.

Mo.

Ill.

Ky.

W. Va.

Va.

Finish –
VIRGINIA BEACH, VA.
June 28

N

"COAST-TO-COAST '86"

Bill is fifty, and works for IBM as a service technician. While at work his business suit seems to belie his bent for things mechanical. But IBM and its customers have benefited from his skills for twenty-five years. There are few problems Bill can't fix or engineer a way around. He is easy-going and fun to be with. But Lolly and I didn't think he would seriously consider going on such a long trip because he wouldn't be able to get time off.

Bill's wife, Connie, had taught herself to roller skate with such enthusiasm and determination that she won the Women's Esquire Figure Skating national championship in 1984. Then a back injury ended the skating, and biking was out too. Raising kids and the responsibilities of jobs have limited Bill's and Connie's vacation activities, a fact that intensifies Bill's propensity for adventure.

So in the fall of 1985, when we began talking speculatively about riding across America, Bill was eager. The question was, if we should decide to make such a trip, could he get the time off from work? Bill must have had positive thoughts, because he began to ride his bike on the 25-mile round trip to work, leaving early and changing into his suit at the office.

Lolly and I don't have formal jobs. That might sound good at first, but "being your own boss" has its own drawbacks. The work of the self-employed doesn't proceed at all during their absence. As self-employed real estate people, we knew we could just take the time if we really wanted to. We'd done it before, in the summer of 1984 when we backpacked 428 miles through Oregon on the Pacific Crest Trail, a trip of twenty-eight days. At the completion of the hike we were slim, trim and suntanned, with calloused feet and worn-out boots. But the hike brought with it such a sense of accomplishment for me that catching up on work afterwards didn't seem so bad. When our children, Mike and Cindy, were still home, we went on lots of family trips, enthusiastically hiking, hunting, fishing and exploring.

But bicycling across the country was an entirely different thing. The logistics alone staggered my mind and I knew I was not realistically assessing the magnitude of the undertaking when we talked about it. After all, Lolly is fifty and I am fifty-three; the hills are steeper than they used to be.

"We're not getting any younger," Lolly would reason.

Of course you can't argue with that, but whether or not it is a sound reason for taking off on a 4,000-mile bicycle ride is highly questionable. We played with the idea, testing each other's reaction to it. Before we knew it, riding across America wasn't just a hazy idea we might think about from time to time; we found ourselves talking about it often. I don't think we were facing squarely the question of whether or not to make the ride; we were talking around the decision. Were we capable of making such a ride? We both thought so, but how about the sore hands and bottoms we had experienced before? We talked about just the two of us possibly going if Bill couldn't make it.

We didn't want to mention the ride to anyone and create any pressure on ourselves that might affect our decision. Instead we read bike touring books, and found these stories exciting. We talked about what we might take along if we went, and what we thought the ride would be like. One thing for sure: it would be physically demanding. Did we want to work that hard? Could we stand up to the rigors of such a trip?

Then, almost defensively, we started to think of reasons why we *should* make the trip. We had driven to the east coast in 1976 with Mike and Cindy and had lots of fun camping our way across the country. That same year—just ten years ago—hundreds of young people made the ride across, organized by Bikecentennial. Lolly feels strongly that exercise and conditioning are beneficial to mental and physical health. I know this is true, but find it hard to take time to keep fit when I am doing other things. Thanks mainly to Lolly's encouragement, we have both stayed in good shape. But lots of the people we know, even young people, aren't in good condition. If we could ride across America, would this inspire anyone to keep in better condition? If we set the goal of riding across the country and made it, would our ride help any of the youngsters we knew realize that they, too, could succeed if they set a goal? It was perhaps lofty speculation, but if just one person was helped to find a new direction, the ride was worth doing.

You meet adventuresome people when you do adventuresome things. Our close friends Ross and Susie Miles would not be part of our lives if we hadn't met Ross thirty-four years ago on a fishing trip. Lots of people are envious of those who do unusual things, but not quite envious enough to put out the effort to do that unusual thing themselves. Others enjoy associating with those who do, or are going to do, adventurous things. "Gee, I wish I could do something like that!" was a comment we had heard often in the past. Meeting new people, making new friends, and seeing new places would be the exciting part of the ride, we decided.

Lolly and I are drawn to challenges like moths to the porch light. The physical challenges were unquestionably daunting. How about the logistics? Could we plan ahead of time and take along everything necessary to make the trip? In my mind I could see bicycles so loaded down with gear we couldn't ride them. Could we adjust, improvise, make do and be flexible when things went wrong?

How would we three react to the stresses of being constantly together? In this respect the ride was like an expedition and we would need to make extra effort to be compatible. Our enthusiasm for the ride finally pushed all negative aspects to one side. We would go, most of all, because we wanted to go.

It was a giddy feeling, being able to talk to others about the trip once the decision had been made. Any doubts about our ability we kept to ourselves. Lolly's mother and my folks, who still think of us as "the kids," all thought it was a great idea. My dad used to ride a lot when he was young, and he was enthusiastic about the trip but worried about us being on the highways in modern, high-speed traffic. Our kids, who think of us in ways sometimes unknown to us, were all for it. Bill became an enthusiastic planner and a strong promoter of the trip. He was continually working on his bike, making improvements and upgrades, evaluating its suitability for a 4,000-plus-mile ride. Lolly and I could tell Bill was holding back, though, not wanting to be too disappointed if he couldn't go.

Florence, a close friend in her sixties who rides her bike every day, gave us tips she had picked up on many short tours in the past. Our friends Carl and Bev, who own a local bike shop, grew awfully tired of our questions about pannier bags, racks, the best gearing and a thousand and one other things. We talked to acquaintances Bill Yeoman and Stan Moore, who were just kids in 1976 when they rode from Oregon to Montreal to watch the Olympics. Stan firmly recommended using lightweight fenders so water wouldn't spray up from the tires so much.

When should we leave? Bill had told us that if he was successful in getting time off, it wouldn't be more than sixty days. Our town, Ashland, holds a traditional Fourth of July parade and festivities that draw participants from a wide area, and we didn't want to miss it. So we could make the ride either before the Fourth, or leave right after. *After* would mean crossing the deserts in July and August, and that didn't seem like a good idea. That made it easy, then; we decided to leave the Oregon coast on May 4. It would be early for crossing the Cascades and Rockies, but we would have to cope. Having set a date made the planning easier, and when friends asked, "When are you leaving?" we could tell them. We still didn't know if Bill could go.

Lolly and I decided to do a "century" one Saturday in October, a ride of 100 miles in one day. Without much planning we left home around 10:00 in the morning and three hours later we were in Grants Pass, 50 miles away. We had lunch and started back, when I began to get tendinitis in my knee and had to slow down. Obviously more conditioning was necessary. Then, late in the afternoon, I had a flat. It was our first experience patching flats on the road. The puncture was from a pushpin, the kind with colored plastic heads used on bulletin boards. We rode the last hour in semi-darkness, and that evening my knee pained so much I could hardly walk. What would a two-month, 4,000-mile ride be like, I wondered?

It doesn't rain all the time in our part of Oregon. Fall is a time of year when foothills and creek bottoms are a kaleidoscope of yellow and red leaves, crunchy underfoot during warm days and limp with dew or frost in early mornings. It was the ideal time to train, so we rode from our home into town and back almost daily. The 20-mile round trip was a pleasure if you don't count saddle soreness. Lolly does volunteer mail delivery for the city, and she began riding her bike into town and on her delivery rounds. I managed to set aside time for riding several times a week. Bill was riding his bike to work every chance he got, and we were all beginning to notice extra muscles in our legs. Our seats, though, didn't seem to get any tougher.

Winter just about stopped our conditioning until Lolly came home with a wind trainer, a frame for mounting a bicycle on rollers that turn a small fan for resistance. Depending upon the gearing of the bicycle, you can enjoy an easy session on the trainer, or increase the effort enough to exhaust a triathlete. Thirty minutes on the trainer really made us perspire, so we draped towels over the bike frame to catch the dripping perspiration. Because time seemed to pass so slowly, we attached a book rack to the handlebars and read while pedaling. I really did want to be in condition when May 4 came around, but it still took a lot of discipline for me to work out on that trainer.

We joined the Bikecentennial organization, a move that made us feel like pros, and also enabled us to buy club maps of the suggested coast-to-coast route. These maps are a series of small segments of the route, with many segments printed on one large sheet. Twelve sheets make up the entire set, but when our order came, only nine sheets were delivered. Our route was still a mystery from Kansas eastward, but the other three maps arrived before we left.

We ended up reading every bicycle touring book we could find. Visualizing our trip was something we found ourselves doing often, but even so the time seemed to drag by. I studied bike repair handbooks so I would be able to give Bill a hand, or do it myself in the event Bill couldn't come along. As we repeatedly visualized our riding routine, we each made lists of the equipment we would need. We knew we were the only propelling power and there was a limit to what our muscles could do, so we tried to be very weight-conscious and avoid duplication.

Cycling clothing manufacturers pay lots of attention to fashion, but we felt many riding jerseys didn't have the high visibility necessary for safety. We visited many bike shops in different areas, and pored over catalogs, and finally gathered suitable clothing. We knew our Gore-tex rain gear would double as excellent wind shells. We found special touring shoes that eased pedaling stresses on our feet while still being limber enough so we could walk comfortably. That meant we could get by on one pair of shoes apiece. Gradually, some of the tips we had received from experienced riders began to make more sense, and we felt encouraged that we were beginning to understand cycling a little better.

Spring weather arrived and we could ride outdoors again. On our first ride into town, wearing our new, brilliant yellow rain gear, I narrowly escaped disaster. I was riding along the right side of the street when a car passed from behind, and then abruptly turned right a few feet in front of me. There was no place to go, so I laid the bike down and slid along the abrasive concrete curb in an effort to stop before hitting the car. The driver was cited, and no permanent harm was done except to my clothing, which was ruined. This was our first real demonstration that many drivers do not see, or allow for, bike riders. It left me jittery and with scabby knees and elbows.

One day a reporter for the local newspaper called, and we agreed to an interview. We spent a pleasant evening at Bill's home talking with Mark Klaas, the sports editor. Mark wanted pictures, so at noon the next day we shivered for a while posing in our summer riding outfits for the photographer. The article was well received, and we were surprised to be in the local limelight. Many friends called, and lots of people would stop Lolly on the street or while she was delivering the city mail, and ask her about the trip. It was great to see the enthusiasm the trip was generating.

A larger newspaper in a nearby town did another article. Now the entire county knew about our ride. Both reporters were young, and had stressed the fact that we were over fifty. Through each piece ran an undercurrent of skepticism about our finishing the ride. Bill had told Mark that a 4,000-mile ride was just a matter of making ten rides like the one down the Oregon coast, end to end. The thread of doubt in the articles just made us more determined. There was no way *we* were going to start doubting now.

An eighty-year-old man, a friend of a friend, called us to ask if he could go along on the ride. We heard he was an accomplished rider, and it was hard to tell him no in view of the enthusiasm he had. As gently as I could, I explained to him that we were a family team.

Lolly designed a special logo for the back of our jerseys. The outline

map of the U.S. had the words "Coast to Coast '86" across it. The t in
"to" was done to depict a religious cross, and Lolly had a local shop
silkscreen the design onto several of our jerseys.

When a local bike club, the Siskiyou Wheelmen, held a century ride,
the three of us went along. We were awed by so many riders in bright,
skin-tight clothing, on prestige name bikes. Then everyone was off from
the starting point in a crowd that rapidly thinned out on the 2-mile hill
leading out of town. By the time we reached the top we were almost last,
and could barely see the next rider in front. I felt disappointed at how
slow we were. But at the top of that hill, Lolly and I decided it was now
or never. I leaned far forward and started driving down the hill as hard
as I could, looking in my mirror to see if Lolly was following. She was
tucked close to my rear wheel, letting me break the wind, her face tight
with exertion. Within a few miles we caught the rider ahead, passed,
and then caught another. Soon we were in the company of several riders
and I, too, could find a windbreak. It was our introduction to drafting,
and without this teamwork we wouldn't have been able to finish the 100
miles in eight hours. We were ecstatic; we could still walk. On the way
home we had car trouble, and had to unload the bikes and ride another 5
miles.

Lolly had been sitting at the dining room table all evening again,
reviewing our route on the maps.

"We'll have to ride at least 70 miles a day," she said suddenly.

I looked up. That didn't sound bad: after all, we had just ridden 100
miles in one day. Then Lolly went ahead and marked all of our route
maps with a red dot where we would be at the end of each day if we rode
70 miles. She enjoyed working with the maps. I enrolled in a night class
in photography.

Bill's anticipation was marred somewhat by not really knowing if he
could go. Characteristically, he didn't mention it much. Then, unexpectedly, IBM issued a directive requiring all employees who had excess
sick or vacation time to use it in 1986. That clinched our decision. Bill's
request for sixty days off was granted. He was delighted, and acted as if
he'd known it would work out all the time.

Since we wanted to be self-sufficient, we would need sleeping bags
and tents. We could stay in motels if the weather was bad and motels
were available. Our backpacking gear was light, and seemed ideal. We
would need a stove, utensils and food. We made a big pile of equipment
on the spare bedroom floor so we could see all of the items. We had no
intention of riding after dark, but what if we were caught out? Head and
tail lights went onto the pile. Soon the mound was huge. Lolly and I
looked at each other, and at the pannier bags into which it must be
packed. I was sure she was including some things we could do without,

and she must have felt the same way about some of my things. I coordinated the tool list with Bill to avoid taking duplicates.

Several people each day asked us about the trip. We didn't realize there would be so much interest, but we were pleased to see increased attention to bike riding in general. We did a thirty-minute radio talk show at the request of the station, and ran out of time. Questions from reporters and friends would fall into two areas: Were we really going to go; and once we left, did we think we would make it?

An interview on television with a reporter who was genuinely interested in biking had us riding along paths in the park in our "Coast to Coast" jerseys. We talked up the trip and the sport of bicycling. Lolly mentioned her ideas on physical fitness, and came across as especially sincere and confident. It was exciting to be doing something to promote bicycling.

Lolly now required twice the time to do her mail route, because everyone wanted to talk about the trip. City hall employees grew accustomed to seeing her in her riding shorts. We continued to receive phone calls from people who wanted to go with us, and as tactfully as I could, I said no. I was also hastily completing some business arrangements. Time was growing short.

Then Bill, looking at his bike with a critical mechanic's eye, decided to rebuild it on a new frame. That made Lolly and me examine our own bikes, and we ended up ordering new touring bikes from the shop. After they arrived, we only had time for a few shakedown rides to get used to the new handling. The stronger, more sensitive bikes were thoroughbreds. Lolly took to hers readily, but I was wobbling all over the road for several hundred miles before growing accustomed to mine.

We made last-minute checks of gear, fearful of forgetting something we would need along a lonely stretch of road. I began to feel like a kid waiting for Santa Claus. At the same time, it dawned on me that we really *were* about to start out on a long, dangerous and difficult trip. Was it wise to do this thing, to expose ourselves to the hazards of traffic and who knew what else?

Lolly made stuff sacks for our sleeping bags out of bright, fluorescent orange material for good visibility. We tried packing all our gear into the rear pannier bags and found that carrying all the weight over the rear wheel made the bikes so unsteady they would shimmy. So we installed front panniers, low on either side of the front wheel, on my bike and Bill's. The shimmy disappeared.

The new panniers provided more room, but we resisted the temptation to take more gear. The bikes were heavy enough already, a lot different from riding bare-bike. With steadiness restored, there was nothing more to do to get ready. May 4 was only two days away.

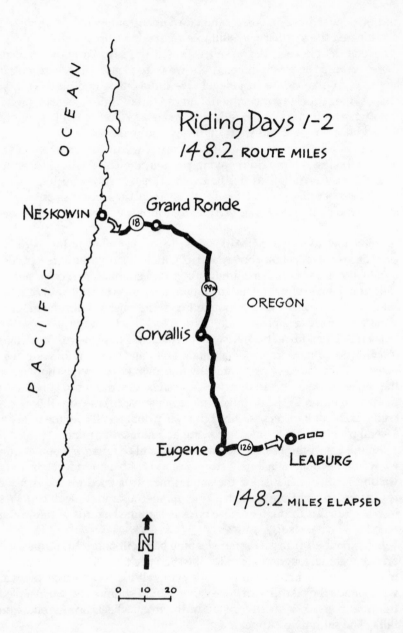

Riding Days 1-2
148.2 ROUTE MILES

OCEAN

PACIFIC

NESKOWIN

Grand Ronde

18

99w

OREGON

Corvallis

Eugene 126 ⟹ LEABURG

148.2 MILES ELAPSED

N

0   10   20

# 3

# LEAVING IS THE HARDEST PART

## NESKOWIN, OREGON–LEABURG, OREGON

The bikes looked frail and vulnerable leaning against the car. At home their slim, polished frames and strong brakes, their silvery rims and hubs and flashing spokes had made them seem so sturdy and dependable. But not now. We were stopped in a wide, paved area near the little coastal town of Neskowin where a dry spot between the puddles on the pavement looked like a good place to load the bikes. We were to meet Bill here to start our ride.

But this wasn't the way I had imagined our departure was going to be. In contrast to the romantic anticipation we had enjoyed during the planning stages, a growing sense of foreboding about the trip spread through me. It had rained last night, and the forecasts were not good. The heavy feeling in the pit of my stomach didn't want to go away, even though I was excited to be nearing the start of the ride.

We had driven to Neskowin the day before in weather so beautiful that the spring foliage, the coast with waves foaming white onto the beach, the gulls wheeling overhead in ever-changing displays of white against azure, were all burned into our memories. Close friends Jo Widness and Betty Kimball, coaches and physical-education instructors in Ashland, accompanied us. At Depoe Bay, we watched white-hulled fishing boats leave a plunging open ocean to navigate the narrow channel into the smooth harbor. It was pleasant riding in the car, even though the springs were sagging a notch from all our gear in the back. Loading the car, I had seen for the first time all of our gear in one place, and the bulk and heft of it was threatening. Would we be able to pedal all that stuff across America?

My mind wandered over our route, which started on the coast, then crossed Oregon and Idaho to Missoula, Montana, before turning south across Wyoming to southeastern Colorado, where it veered east to our destination at Virginia Beach, Virginia. Driving along, I could easily visualize the colored line Lolly had drawn across the United States map. On a day like this it seemed making the ride would be easy. To celebrate the eve of our departure, we had a seafood dinner in a restaurant overlooking the bay in Lincoln City.

I took the gear from the car and, to occupy my mind, began fastening the panniers in place. Yes, it was going to be a wet day. How would the loaded bikes react on the slippery pavement? Maybe one of us would crash and the trip would have to be cut short. I pulled the pannier lashing tight and tried to dispel such thoughts. I was feeling the excitement now, and my adrenaline was flowing. Lolly was loading her bike and I could tell she was excited too. But the nagging concern continued. Are we doing the right thing, I wondered? I'd had no doubts while we were planning the trip. Sure, the training and conditioning had been hard, but usually we had enjoyed good weather, nothing at all like today's. I ignored the unfriendly aura that seemed to be settling over the place and strapped on my sleeping bag.

This morning had dawned with an uncertain sun peeking through scattered clouds with barely enough warmth to burn away wisps of coastal fog that now hung menacingly in a dense bank, just beyond the surf line. Soon the clouds were taking turns blocking the sun completely.

We found a cafe and stuffed ourselves with pancakes, thinking we would need the carbohydrates for fuel.

Connie and Bill arrived then. I was assured by Bill's calm, relaxed manner until I saw his hand shaking as he strapped the load on his bike. He was affected too. Even Lolly, usually enthusiastic and ready to take on anything, was strangely quiet. Our moment of truth was at hand. The leaning bikes, their fluorescent orange loads bright against the blue of the car, looked top heavy. I knew we had to make the commitment. Slowly, almost awkwardly, we climbed on.

We rode to the beach while Connie, Jo and Betty walked, and pushed the bikes out through the loose sand to the line of froth where thin, shiny wave remnants skimmed up the beach and sank. The sun came out, making the long johns we wore suddenly too warm. Connie and Jo took pictures of us, helmets and all. (They show us somewhat dazzled, oblivious to the beauty of the beach, and to the rocky, pine-crowned promontory south of us jutting protectively out into the ocean.) We probably stayed on the beach longer than necessary, and I don't remember what we said to Connie and Jo and Betty when we got back to the road. It both hurt and felt strange to turn our backs on loved ones. The realization that we were about to leave our familiar lifestyle was scary. It was very quiet as we rode out onto the highway.

Noon rush hour found us, after a strenuous morning crossing 30 miles of the coast range mountains, at the Corridor Cafe in Grande Ronde. Lolly looked at the two battered pickups parked near, one with the bed piled full of junk, and seemed unwilling to leave the bikes. "Let's use our cable locks," she said.

Bill nodded and secured our bikes to the porch railings with the long cable we had brought along. Wallets and cameras were in our left-front pannier bags, so we unhooked them and carrying our helmets walked self-consciously into the cafe. Everyone near us stopped talking at the same time—all, that is, except the pretty, exuberant young waitress, who came right over and smiled.

"Where ya from?" she asked.

"We're from Ashland," Lolly said.

The girl's face lit up. "I've been to Ashland to see the Shakespeare plays." Then she asked, "Where ya goin'?"

Lolly gulped and hesitated just a little. "To the east coast."

Her declaration did something positive for our spirits, and it also helped the other diners lose their shyness. They began to question us, keeping us so busy talking that we barely had time to finish the day's second order of pancakes—this one a double. These people are vicarious bikers, I thought; everyone felt like a friend.

The occasional showers we rode through became a downpour as we exited the coast range and turned south into the rolling country of the Willamette Valley, where small hills a few hundred feet high extended as forested ridges down to the grain ranches in the valley to spar for territory. Ranch homes sat on knolls, surveying their domains of cropland, sheltered by groves of oak and Douglas fir.

"I'm getting wet," Lolly complained. "Time for shoe covers."

We were heading for Corvallis, where Connie and her son Ron were to meet us that evening. We had our rain gear on already, but we stopped to add the waterproof shoe covers. Even so, driving rain and spray from puddles soaked our feet. Then, with a flash of lightning, heavy machine-gun drops splashed onto the pavement faster than the water could run off, forcing us to ride through the equivalent of an endless puddle. The rain turned to hail abruptly, treating us to the unique sound of hailstones on our riding helmets. It's like having your head inside a bucket while someone throws gravel at you.

By the time we reached Lewisburg, a combination store and gas station at a crossroads, we were shivering from the near-freezing air and our wet hands and feet. "I'm stopping here to get warm," Lolly said.

One quick look at us and the owner, a bearded man about forty, pointed towards some doughnuts on the counter.

"I can make some hot chocolate in the microwave," he offered.

We must have looked pretty miserable judging from the way the storekeeper reacted. Soon we were holding cups of hot liquid, warming our hands and taking cautious sips. After asking about our destination, the owner began telling us about his store and how he had increased business by putting in a machine to cook chicken. As we stopped shivering and took a good look around, we saw pictures and trophies he had won in four-wheel-drive racing adorning the walls. The conversation turned quickly to the sport, and it was obvious that the storekeeper was a fanatic.

"I run the store to get the money to race," he said simply.

Well, I thought, we sure understand that kind of priority: here *we* are taking time off to ride across the country. As we paid and thanked him for his kindness, we felt kinship for the man who had genuinely tried to be helpful, a man who knew what he wanted to do and was enjoying doing it.

The Tau Kappa Epsilon fraternity in Corvallis where Ron lives was an even 80 miles from where we started that morning. Connie and Ron were there waiting, and we all went to dinner. The booths in the restaurant seemed hard, but I knew it was because my seat was sore from the long hours on the bicycle. Despite Lolly's weariness, I could tell she wasn't comfortable sitting down either. But we felt elated. We had just completed a long day, with heavily loaded bikes, and somehow it was a real thrill. Maybe we had been operating all day on excitement, on adrenaline because it was the first day; probably this kind of energy boost at the end of the day would wear off. But for now, sitting safe in a warm restaurant and enjoying the food, we could luxuriate in the feeling of being "on tour." I hoped the feeling would stick with us.

That evening, Bob Foley, manager at the TKE house, offered us the use of his apartment, an offer we hesitated to accept until we learned it would give him a chance to stay at his place out in the country. Our presence didn't seem to change the pattern of life in the fraternity house at all, and before we left the next morning we had the chance to meet most of the fellows. They had heard about our trip from Ron, and had encouraging words for us. A couple of the guys were serious bike riders and posed thoughtful questions. Then we said good-bye to Ron and Connie.

The second day seemed to me more like the real beginning of the trip. We were truly on our own now, with no predetermined destination, not knowing who we would meet or where we would be at the end of this day. Sure, the first day had given us a taste of tour riding, but it had held little uncertainty. Today was different.

A stiff headwind developed early to accompany the showery weather as we rode south through the Willamette Valley, and I began to have trouble with tendinitis in my knee. Soon I was unable to lead because of the pain, and Lolly and Bill alternated in the lead position while I drafted. An elastic foam knee brace helped some, but I just couldn't keep up our regular pace. I wasn't enjoying the countryside at all, riding along with my head down and my teeth clenched, oblivious to the sweeping oxbow loops of the Willamette River, the grass-seed farms, orchards and nut ranches. I just wanted the day to end.

Lolly noticed the broken spoke because of a wobble in Bill's rear wheel as we rode by a pretentious ranch house in the rain. Buildings and sheds stretched for hundreds of feet, and looked like great places to work on the bike. The woman who answered the door stared at me as if I were from outer space, and when I requested the use of a shed to do some repairs she said to ask her husband who was working in the shop.

The sound of a grinder guided me to the well-equipped, heated shop where a radio was playing. No one responded to my knock, so I stuck my head in the door.

"Anybody here?"

A sleek, shiny '67 Corvette occupied the center of the shop like a polished trophy on a pedestal. Not a speck of dust appeared on the car, restoration work was nearly finished, and the whole place looked so clean you could eat from the floor. It was apparent from the look on the farmer's face that he didn't want to be interrupted, but he did give his permission to use the shed.

We shared the protecting roof with a gleaming John Deere tractor and a big combine, and tackled the spoke. I don't think Bill had ever changed a spoke before, but he went at it as if he knew what he was doing. Unpack the bike, off with the rear wheel, remove the rear sprocket cluster, replace the spoke and then reverse the process. In less than thirty minutes we were stuffing arms and legs back into clammy rain gear. The farmer had never left his shop.

That headwind was still blowing, coming straight down the road at us. Many people think hills are the worst thing a cyclist encounters. "How do you get up those hills?" they invariably ask. But any experienced rider knows it is not hills but headwinds that he dreads. Oh, hills can be steep, sometimes very steep, but all hills have summits. You can ride up hills slowly, or you can zigzag to cut down the percent of grade. Hills are usually only a few miles in length, and offer a coast down the other side to make up for the time and effort spent climbing them. But headwinds, if strong or constant, give no chance to rest. They are a continuous force that must be constantly overcome in order to move forward.

"No, sixty-five dollars is the price."

The owner of the bike shop in Eugene, Oregon, indicated the tag on the part we were inspecting. The price seemed high, but my hints were being ignored and I wasn't accomplishing anything toward getting the price reduced.

"Can you install it right away?" I asked.

"Yes," replied the owner, "we'll have you on your way again in thirty minutes."

"Okay." Good service that saved us time was important too, I rationalized.

Lolly had been experiencing some instability with her bike, and we thought it was because of too much weight in the handlebar bag she carried. This bike shop sold front panniers and racks, like those Bill and I used. While we were picking out bags to fit the racks, a man wearing full riding regalia entered the shop and right away he spotted our loaded touring bikes. He appeared to be in his fifties, with a well-trimmed beard and graying hair.

"Where are you from?" he asked pleasantly.

"We started yesterday at Neskowin, and we're headed for the east coast," I answered.

I wasn't sure if the expression on his face was envy or admiration, but he looked our bikes over carefully again and paused before replying, as if gauging our ages. A faraway look came into his eyes.

"I have to work," he said. "I can't take that much time off."

Then he volunteered to lead us through the confusing maze downtown, where miles of jogging and bike paths have earned Eugene the nickname of "The Running Town." We followed our guide through the traffic, near the University of Oregon, barely able to keep up the pace he was setting with his unladen bike. Evidently he was busy proving, probably unconsciously and to himself, that he too had what it takes to make a cross-country trip. He rode as if he had a lot more experience than we did. When he finally stopped in the middle of a bike-path bridge crossing the Willamette, his wave and smile were sincere—and wistful. We never did learn his name.

It was hot-chocolate-and-three-doughnuts-apiece weather as we rode up the McKenzie River drainage towards the foothills of the Cascades.

Suburbia gave way to occasional commuter population, which in turn thinned and gave way to forest. Open fields became smaller. Lolly checked the map and suggested Leaburg, one of those towns shown in the smallest print imaginable on the map, as a likely destination for the night. It was raining on us occasionally and getting late when we stopped to eat at a country restaurant. We got the usual stares, and I guess our long johns under our shorts and jerseys did look funny. Bill wasn't helping appearances much by wearing his long johns over his shorts. By the time we finished eating it was dark, so we clipped on our flashing tail lights.

Thirty minutes later as we reached Leaburg it was pitch black and raining hard. Motel prospects didn't look good, and a flashlight check of the map showed no campgrounds nearby. We didn't really want to camp in the rain anyway, and we certainly didn't want to ride any farther at night in the rain.

The roar of machinery directed our attention across the highway, where lights shone through a piece of plastic hung over the door of a garage. I went over and walked around the edge of the plastic. A bearded young man wearing the boots, heavy pants and suspenders of a logger was busy sandblasting rust off the rear bumper of his pickup. He turned off the dusty, hissing machine, and listened as we asked about a place to stay.

"Well," he said thoughtfully, "you can set up your tents in the school yard across the street. Won't hurt a thing. Or, if you want, maybe you can rent the gymnasium."

"The gymnasium?" At first I thought I hadn't heard him right. The rain was falling harder now.

"Yes, just see Gordon Vance, our mayor. He handles renting the gymnasium. The ladies' exercise class is using it right now, but they get through at 8:30."

Not unusual in small towns, I thought: everyone knows what everyone else is doing. If the exercise class was about to finish with the gymnasium, it was worth investigating. Any roof over our heads sounded inviting. We thanked the logger in the roar of the re-started sandblaster, rode up the gravel road he had indicated, found Gordon's house, and knocked on the door. Yes, the gymnasium could be rented for ten or fifteen dollars, and the ladies would be through by now. Since Gordon seemed to be leaving the fee up to me, I chose the ten-dollar figure, and paid him.

Mayor Vance got his flashlight and walked down to the gym while we rode our bikes around on the road and met him at the door. Unlocking it, he pointed out several banks of bright overhead lights; it would be easy to burn lots of electricity. He showed us how to turn the lights on and off—especially off.

"Don't use more light than you have to," Gordon asked, "and be sure to lock the door when you leave in the morning."

Then he left us standing inside the 5,000-square-foot gymnasium, out on the basketball court, staring at each other in the brilliance of one set of overhead lights. We were warm, it was dry, and we looked at each other and suddenly started to laugh. With a men's and a women's restroom, a kitchen and any number of choices to sleep, this seemed an unlikely place for three transcontinental cyclists. Lolly claimed a long, heavily padded table for her sleeping bag. Bill and I chose the floor. We took pictures of our corner of the gym, washed, and wrote in our logs while the rain pounded against the roof. Our second day was ending in a gymnasium. We looped our cable through the handles when the doors wouldn't lock from inside. I was fast slipping into the sleep of the really tired when Bill said dryly, "On a square-foot basis, this might be our best lodging buy of the trip."

Yes, I thought, it might be. And after my knee quit hurting during the afternoon, it hadn't been too bad. We had proven during the last two days that we could ride the necessary distance, even with the heavy loads on our bikes. And we had already met several interesting and unusual people, one of the rewards of the trip we had promised ourselves. Things seemed to be going pretty well. Maybe, I thought sleepily, I had overestimated the hardships of the ride.

# 4

# *LOGGERS EAT*
# *BIGGER PANCAKES*

## LEABURG, OREGON–CAMBRIDGE, IDAHO

The snow began sticking to the road before we reached the summit of the Cascades, at first as a barely discernible graying of the pavement but changing with alarming rapidity to a slushy white layer that made riding treacherous. I was near exhaustion after a long day of uphill grades that had led to this 4,800-foot pass. We stopped to put on gloves, shoe covers and Gore-tex, and it didn't take a fortune-teller to see that Lolly and Bill were not only tired but apprehensive. We were a half mile short of the summit.

"We can't stay here," I said. "We've got to go on over the top and get below the snow."

The wind was whistling, swirling the snow around us in a fading light made more ominous by the storm. As we rode on towards the summit, I could see the tire tracks behind us cutting through to the pavement. At least it wasn't icy yet, but how long would that small favor continue? Even at our slow pace, we had to squint to keep the snow out of our eyes.

We were a cold, shaking and worried trio as we reached the summit. After the exertion of the climb, our body heat was dropping rapidly. Snow remaining from winter, a couple of feet deep, stretched into the forest on either side of the road. We had to keep our speed down because of the snow on the pavement. The slope was so gentle the elevation was not decreasing very much. But our speed along the top was faster than our climbing speed, and even with the protective gear the wind was cutting, further robbing our bodies of heat. I knew we had to get to a lower elevation, where it was warmer, and do it as quickly as possible.

Finally the downgrade was steep enough that we could coast. Good,

I thought, we're going to make it okay now. There was less snow on the pavement too, but our tires weren't cutting through it as well. It was getting colder, and icy. Bill was in the lead, Lolly was behind me and we were using brakes to keep the speed around 15 miles per hour going down. The bikes were squirrelly on the slippery pavement. Here we are coming down off the pass, I grumbled inwardly, and it's getting worse instead of better.

We heard the truck then, closing rapidly from behind us, jake brakes snapping as it roared down the hill. It was a mass of lights and snow spray in the rearview mirror, and then it was passing, in the opposite lane to give us room, a semi and trailer loaded with lumber. Sanding gravel from the shoulder mixed with swirling snow in the wake of the truck. We were recovering from that when we heard another truck coming.

There was something different about the way the second truck approached. In the mirror he seemed not to be moving over. Then I could see that he was beside Lolly, and she was wavering in the wind blast—God, I thought, he's not giving her much room—and then he was beside me. I heard Lolly shout a warning and as if in a slow-motion bad dream I saw him whip the front wheels to the right. This is not happening, I thought, but it was . . . I sensed the big dual wheels swinging towards my left side—and flew off the jarring drop of the paved shoulder and into loose pumice sanding gravel. The bike swerved and bucked and suddenly I wasn't able to guide it anymore—I could only try to survive the wake of the truck and the gravel. Where's the nearest hospital? I wondered. How bad will it be? The balance point of

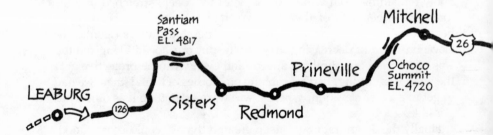

# Riding Days 3-8
## 446.2 ROUTE MILES

the bike kept changing, and as soon as I corrected for that, the wheels would slip to the other side in gravel too loose to support them. Finally, my heart pounding wildly, I had control of the bike and got back on the pavement.

I was furious. The driver had obviously done that intentionally, missing me by a distance equal to his intelligence. And then we heard the third truck. But this rig, also a lumber truck, pulled wide and gave us lots of room.

I was shaking, not so much from the cold now but from the experience. I'd had a good look at the second truck, at a range much closer than I care to think about. I knew I would recognize the truck if I saw it again, the load of lumber had been different from the other two. Bill had seen the excitement in his mirror, and of course it had happened right in front of Lolly. She tried to calm me down, as I was all for hurrying on to the next truck stop, hoping that the truck would be there and I could find the driver.

We coasted down, off the mountain, in the growing darkness. The fury in me let go slowly. We had been well treated by the cars and trucks we had met up until now. We always tried to be responsible riders, keeping single file and to the far right, riding out of the traffic lane on the shoulder if it was paved. As a result, the vehicles we met had been respectful of our space and in fact they often waved and smiled. After three days on the road we had begun to think that coexisting with traffic was a cinch. And then along came that Neanderthal in the truck. What was he trying to prove, anyway? Didn't he realize what could have happened?

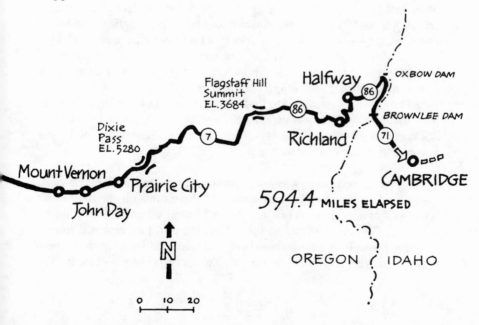

The picture wouldn't leave my mind; those big dual tires, higher than my bicycle seat, two feet away from my left hip pocket and moving towards me fast. The panic swerve to the right, and then the jarring, bucking ride in gravel that was trying to pull me down. And the driver was probably laughing over the whole thing. Were there going to be more drivers like this on the trip? If so, was it really acceptable, being out there on the road unprotected, while three- and four-thousand-pound automobiles passed close by us at high speed? Nothing protected us from that abrasive pavement but our balance. Our helmets would crush like paper upon impact with steel or rubber. Was this trip a good risk? Suppose we met others in vehicles who got some sick thrill out of bullying cyclists?

I was still angry at the truck driver, but as we pedaled along in the dark, our flashing tail lights reflecting strobe-like off the roadside trees, my adrenaline began to wear off. I realized my anger wasn't directed so much at the truck driver but at his ignorance. Endangered by ignorance—what a helpless feeling! As we rode on I began to realize that in all likelihood the truck driver was one of a kind and we could continue the ride in reasonable safety. We would continue to watch in our mirrors, and be ready.

It was ten at night when we rode into Sisters, a picturesque little town at the eastern foot of the Cascades. The motel we stopped at didn't have bathtubs—Lolly likes to soak after a ride—so we ended up at the other end of town where we rented a cabin unit with tub. By that time, the cafes in Sisters had closed and only by the good grace of a storekeeper who opened up just for us were we able to get some cold sandwiches. It was nearly midnight when we got to bed, still numb from the Cascade crossing. I couldn't close my eyes without recalling a sight we had seen that morning—the remains of a deer that had been run over by a truck. Large stains on the pavement, a few shreds of hide and a couple of hooves were all that was left. Shuddering at the vision of those truck tires coming at me, I fell into a troubled sleep.

Next morning we wanted to find a laundromat, but couldn't; we were told that the Sisters sewage system would not allow a laundromat hookup. But the people in Sisters were friendly and the town had been a haven after a day of hardship.

We were in Redmond, Oregon, and the day previous Bill had broken his second spoke. Two broken spokes in three days on the road don't bode well at any time. While Lolly and I found a laundromat Bill had ridden to Greenridge Touring bike shop. We had just rejoined forces.

Peggy Davis had rebuilt the wheel, Bill said. His bike sported a new rear wheel with forty new, shining spokes. I could just picture it: Bill, technician *extraordinaire*, watching as a woman rebuilt the rear wheel of his precious bicycle.

"She did a good job," Bill said. "Gals are often much better bike mechanics than guys."

Well, if Bill said that, I knew that Peggy must have worked with care. We headed east.

While it is your seat that gets sore, you really bicycle on your stomach. We couldn't believe the amount we were eating. Our usual breakfast was pancakes, lots of pancakes, and whatever else we could get with them on the combination special. Eggs and bacon were okay, but it was the pancakes we craved. Psychological, perhaps, but it seemed that our strength in the morning came from pancakes. We began comparing the places we ate at by the size and quality of their pancakes. Oddly enough, as we went eastward, the pancakes were becoming larger. We would have syrup on them once in a while, but found ourselves developing a craving for jelly and jam.

We viewed Prineville, the central Oregon cattle town, mainly as a place to stop and eat. We began eating huge lunches, so big that other patrons would stare at us. And in between the usual three meals, we would stop for at least two more huge snacks. So we were beginning to feel the need for five meals a day, consuming four or five thousand calories. And we were getting hungrier.

The multiple summits of eastern Oregon fell behind slowly. We grew accustomed to the sweaty work of climbing a couple of thousand feet vertically along a six-percent grade; then pulling on the Gore-tex and wind gloves for a coast that never failed to chill us to the bone as we made our descent on the other side. We camped in the Ochoco Mountains, near the summit, up a side canyon in the timber to get out of the cold wind. Dinner here was freeze-dried chicken. No pancakes for breakfast either; instant oatmeal and Tang would have to do. Our water supply ran low, so we boiled water taken from a little ravine. That lasted until we reached the Blueberry Muffin Cafe, in Mitchell.

Many riders have stopped at the Blueberry over the years, and the walls sport lots of postcards from all over the country sent by riders who have been their guests. We took the address and vowed to write. Everyone was so hospitable towards us, and either our riding clothes weren't attracting so much attention or we were growing less self-conscious. We felt even better when, a few miles down the road at Dayville, a well-dressed man in a shiny pickup asked us if we would like to stay at the church-run bike hostel. In the last year the little town hosted over 100 riders.

Mount Vernon, John Day and Prairie City were visited and then left as our singing tires carried us eastward, and then we were in Baker. Seven days of mountain riding had begun to harden our muscles, and we were feeling pretty good, especially during those times when the sun came out.

We were waiting for a red light when a car came alongside.

"Jimmy Day!" Lolly called out. It was a chance meeting of an old friend who we knew lived in Baker. We visited briefly with Jim and his wife Shirley, then had a chance to see Bill and Mary Day, Jim's parents, whom we had known for twenty years. You never know whom you'll meet while waiting at a stoplight.

The Mule Shoe Motel had an office, but no one was there. A hand-written note said to take the keys of room six; someone would collect later. We did that, glad to find any room. As we had ridden into Halfway, the first motel had a "No Vacancy" sign out. It was late in the day, and we had travelled far since leaving Baker: along the Powder River and the route of the Oregon Trail pioneers, and through Richland, a town and surrounding rural area that provide many of the 150 students for the Halfway high school. Halfway is quaint, and a party town.

As we devoured the huge helpings of the prime rib special at the Pioneer Cafe, a couple came over to our table.

"We passed you on the road earlier today," the man said. He was a minister at Newbridge, a tiny settlement nearby.

After that another man stopped at our table. He had passed us near Baker, and again on the hill a few miles back.

"I'm in Halfway for a wedding," he said. "Many of the people around here are my relations. Halfway is a party town—that is, we all come here to get together."

And lively it was. Tomorrow was Mother's Day, and tonight the cafe was packed. Loud music came from the taverns, and cars were parked all over. We wanted to do something to celebrate too, and ended up going to the laundromat and writing our logs. We were 536 miles from home, and feeling well, except that we each had knee pains.

This part of Oregon slopes away to the east to the Snake River, impounded here by Oxbow and Brownlee dams for that brief second of eternity that is forever in mortal time. Cross the river, and you're in Idaho. We celebrated our second state with the Mother's Day special at the Gateway Cafe: pork chops, dressing and strawberry shortcake, reduced price for mothers and the shortcake free. Then, as if to reprimand us for all that fat and protein, the route took us up to over 4,100 feet in 6 miles. We didn't feel well for a few hours after that, but I guess we burned up the food because we didn't forget our afternoon snack.

We discovered George Danielson's General Store more or less by accident. At Cambridge, Idaho, we decided to send home some things we had been carrying with us. We no longer used the helmet radios, and some clothing items we had never worn. Thinking it would help reduce the distress in our knees, we were anxious to reduce the weight we carried as much as possible. Lolly bought a pasteboard box at the post office, and then we looked around for packing material.

"Yes," George Danielson said, "I have some plastic packing material in this box. Take the whole thing, and bring back what you don't need."

George was about seventy, smiled a lot, and was helpful. The store was at least the same age, with pine floors and row after row of counters, filled with everything imaginable. I thanked him, and took the box of packing across the street where Lolly and Bill were getting ready to mail our stuff home. The plastic chaff filled the box nicely.

As I turned toward the store to return the packing, my eye fell on the blue plastic tarp I had purchased earlier. It was intended to keep pannier bags dry when camping so we wouldn't have to keep them inside the tent. But the plastic tarp must have weighed around two pounds, and we hadn't used it. On impulse, I unstrapped it and took it into the general store.

"Thanks," I said, giving the packing to George. "You wouldn't happen to have any really light tarps, would you?" I explained what the use was, and that the tarp I was carrying was too heavy. George thought a minute.

"How about garbage bags?" he asked.

"I don't know, I haven't thought about it." George took off, and I followed him up and down three aisles before he found them, brown plastic bags on a large bulk roll.

"We use these to bag our trash," he said. "They're thirty cents each, and you need two." Before I could object, he tore off two bags, and then took the tarp from me. Two aisles away, he stopped in front of a pile of blue plastic tarps just like the one I had bought.

"Let's see," he said, "I owe you five dollars and forty cents." He plunked the tarp down on the pile with the finality of a trade irrevocably completed.

George's father had started the General Store in 1914, and George had been working in it ever since high school. It was full of goodies, about everything you could imagine, and a lot of it was in bulk, the way things used to be sold. True, some items on the shelf would probably be more suitable for collections than use, and there was a lot of dust about. But that several thousand square feet of space was a treasure house. Whatever you could want, George Danielson probably has it in stock—somewhere.

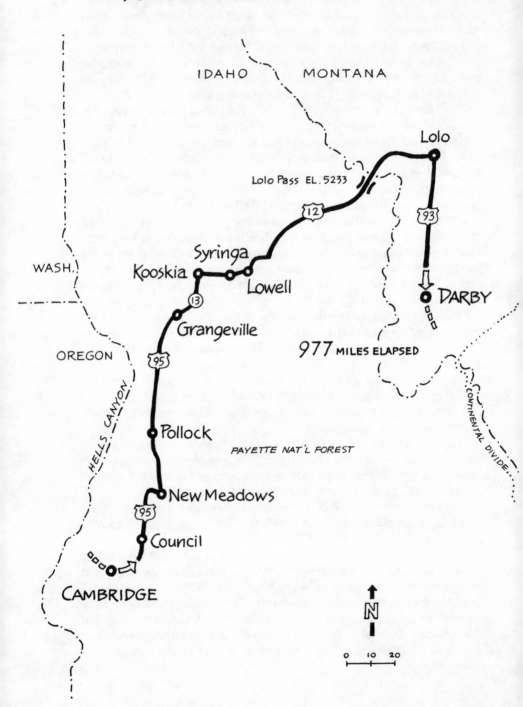

Riding Days 9-14
382.6 ROUTE MILES

IDAHO     MONTANA

Lolo

Lolo Pass EL. 5233

12          93

Syringa
Kooskia        Lowell
WASH.          13

Grangeville        DARBY

OREGON    95        977 MILES ELAPSED

Pollock

PAYETTE NAT'L FOREST

HELLS CANYON

New Meadows
95

Council

CAMBRIDGE

CONTINENTAL DIVIDE

N

0    10    20

*May 12–17*

# 5

# *LEWIS AND CLARK FOLLOWED OUR ROUTE*

CAMBRIDGE, IDAHO—DARBY, MONTANA

One of our reasons for wanting to make the ride had been the opportunity to inspire others. Well, as near as I could determine, after nine days on the road we hadn't inspired anyone. Instead, our knees were killing us each time we came to a hill, and while we were in good shape from a cardiovascular standpoint and our muscles were strong, our seats were sore. The sensations resulting from sitting on a bicycle saddle for ten hours or so cannot be appreciated by the inexperienced. No, we hadn't inspired anyone; well—perhaps because we were ecstatic about the speed we were making—maybe we inspired ourselves just a bit.

We weren't riding a marathon, and didn't want to feel pushed, but we couldn't escape the fact that Bill had to be back home on July 2, fifty-one days from now. When we checked the map, it was impossible not to see the red dot Lolly had put at the end of each theoretical 70-mile day. We were ahead of our average, east of the ninth dot.

It felt good to be able to pedal over mountain passes. We had made a pact not to walk a foot; we would ride the bike every bit of the way or we wouldn't go at all. Now, little more than a week into the trip, we were hardened to the hills and had plenty of muscle power. Except our knees hurt. And our seats hurt. I wondered how long you have to ride before your seat becomes hardened to the ordeal?

We met Carol at the Squaw Creek Campground on the Little Salmon River. An attractive girl, she had her big commercial machine set up out on a grassy spot and was sewing tepee covers. Carol had a sewing shop in McCall, but business had been slow. So slow, she was filling in as off-season operator of the campground, and doing patching work on heavy, board-stiff canvas. She blamed McCall's reliance on tourism for the poor economics; when tourists are few the economy is awful, she told us.

The river rushed by with a muted roar just a few feet away. We set up our tents beside a tepee platform and soon had a driftwood fire going. Lolly was doing laundry, keeping the ancient washer running with a rock propped against the start button. We had called Con, a cousin we hadn't seen in fifteen years, before we reached McCall, where he lived. He had to work until evening and offered to catch up with us at the end of the day wherever we were. Since McCall was a 12-mile-long, 1,000-foot climb off our route, we were grateful for his solution to the problem. We had made good time through Council, New Meadows, and down the river past little known and easily missed spots such as Pinehurst and Pollock, and Con had to drive about 50 miles to catch up with us.

Our visit with Con lasted well into the evening. He had moved his family to McCall from the Silicon Valley several years ago, to be able to raise his kids in a small-town environment. For several years he made a good living, working in a service station he intended to buy. But the economy weakened around 1980, mainly because tourism decreased.

"We're moving to Connecticut," Con stated. "I'm going to complete my masters in vocational education." He was bitter but philosophical. "When a town goes all out for tourist dollars and the tourists don't come, you're in trouble."

Finally the evening ended because Con had to drive back to McCall. He had to work in the morning. In our tent, Lolly and I talked about what Con had said.

"Too bad he has to leave McCall," I said. "He likes it so much."

"Yes, kind of like those people at lunch today."

I thought back to the Pine Ridge Cafe near Tamarack summit east of Council, where we had eaten. Owner Steve Davis had perked up the minute he heard we were from Oregon.

"I was born in Ontario, Oregon," he said. "My grandfather was one of the town's early settlers. I married Maxine there, and our children were born there." He was leading up to something. "A few years ago, we took our savings and made a down payment on a parcel of land. It was okay to build on it when we bought it, but a short time later the LCDC wouldn't let us build a home on our own land. That's when we left Oregon for good and came to Idaho. We'll never go back."

Lying in the tent listening to the river rushing by, I thought about how many times I had heard similar stories about Oregon. Land-use planning has many facets, of course—but oh, how many people have been needlessly damaged. Then the symphony of the river interrupted, at least what I used to enjoy as a symphony, the subtle notes of currents and the gurgle of eddies blending into an orchestra of subtle yet relentless power. The individual instruments are not quite so clear to my ears now. Soon the song of the river took over, and fatigue did the rest.

Eight switchbacks on the old highway makes climbing White Bird Pass from the Salmon River an impressive, almost classic ride. We enjoyed spotty sunshine and, even more important, a strong tailwind that helped us up the grade. Two whitetail deer bounded up a brushy draw, their flags conspicuous against the green of the hillside. We took time to read historical plaques on monuments to the Nez Perce war, knowing we could depend upon the wind for a boost up the hill when we started again. Finally we were near the top, where the old road intersected a newer route cut along the side of the mountain. Here, close to the summit, the wind was very strong and gusty. We turned onto the new road, and continued upwards on a section cut deeply across a ridge.

I was leading when we came out of the cut onto the fill, and suddenly the unexpected wind shear hit. I was going about 6 or 7 miles an hour when it hit on the left side, turning the front wheel to the right and— wham! I ran straight into the steel guard rail at right angles.

Lolly and Bill, following behind and not yet out into the wind, really broke up over that one. I could imagine how it must have looked, but I couldn't help it; the wind was strong. Besides, even at slow speed the impact had been jarring and not a bit funny. I got the bike straightened out, climbed on, and managed to get moving again. Lolly came out into the wind and it stopped her cold: she put her feet on the pavement to hold the bike up. I could watch her easily—because my front wheel was jammed into the guard rail a second time. I heard plenty of taunts about my riding the rest of the way to the top.

We armored up against downhill chill and eased over. The gusty wind continued, only now we were coasting, and much more vulnerable to a crash. Cautiously, under constant braking, we moved down the mountain. Lolly was going very slow, her face white with the strain.

"Careful!" Bill called.

We had to pass alternately between sheltering cut banks and fills open to violent wind gusts. It was terrifying because sometimes the gusts were unpredictable; you just had to hold on and be ready. This is wrong, I thought. Going downhill is supposed to be fun.

When the view opened up to the north, the whole valley below was invisible, filled with a pall of blowing dust. The wind chauffeured us into Grangeville under a weak sun, and a few ominous snowflakes from somewhere zipped by. The dust storm and wind were the talk of the town, but we were more interested in the excellent Mexican dinner we had at the Charcoal Broiler restaurant. Even though our motel was built of concrete block, we could still hear the wind whistling late that night.

"WARNING BICYCLISTS," the sign near Kooskia said. "DANGEROUS TRUCK TRAFFIC AND NARROW ROAD NEXT 100 MILES. TAKE ALTERNATE ROUTE." A check of the map showed no alternate route, at least not from here, not without backtracking a whole basketful of miles. And we were not going to do that. We would have to be careful, that's all. My stomach tightened as I remembered the lumber truck on Santiam Pass. Our map had indicated heavy truck traffic on this section, but somehow the sign looked so much more authoritative. Well, we were committed now. As we rode on, I noticed that the road had no shoulder, and the lane was narrow.

We sneaked past the settlement of Syringa and on into Lowell, where we filled our water bottles near a sign that said, "NO SERVICES NEXT 68 MILES." We had food and camping gear, so services weren't a problem, but how about the trucks? What were we getting into? The road was narrow, and many times the right side of the lane ended tight against a guard rail, or a drop-off into the river. There was no room to get off the road.

The truck traffic began to pick up a little, but all of the drivers were courteous. And then, when I swerved to go around a small rock while a truck was approaching from behind, we noticed something. Apparently interpreting my swerve as wobbling lack of control, the truck slowed abruptly and moved halfway into the opposite lane before passing us. From then on, if we were in a spot where we could not get out of the traffic lane, one of us would wobble around a bit when we saw a vehicle overtaking from behind. This maneuver usually had the effect of providing many extra feet of clearance as we were passed. Since our rearview mirrors were wide angle, they had a tendency to compress distance, and we had to be careful in judging how far away a passing car or truck actually was, and how fast it was going. But the wobble maneuver worked.

At highway speed in an auto, you don't even notice places like Syringa, Stites or Lowell. To a cyclist, however, even the smallest settlement takes on a definite character of its own. I can't say exactly what creates the impression; I suppose it's the way structures are maintained and what is lying around, and what types of businesses are thriving and a whole lot of other subtle things like the way the people react to us. But halfway through any small town or area, we had a good idea of the character of its people. Time after time, as we stopped in a cafe or store, we would see our first impressions confirmed.

Riding up the Clearwater River and its tributary, the Lochsa, was pleasant because the sun was out much of the time and we could enjoy the beauty of the area. The huge Selway-Bitterroot Wilderness begins at the river, and narrow suspension bridges at trailheads give hiker and equestrian access to the heavily timbered region.

Lolly would usually ride in the rear position while Bill and I took turns in the lead. We had developed protective systems to warn each other of hazards. Since Lolly had the best view to the rear, she would shout "Car behind!" each time she spotted an auto closing from the rear. Whoever was leading would warn "Car ahead!" if a vehicle was approaching from the opposite direction. In this way we could quickly assimilate any traffic hazard. After a few days of hearing "Car behind!" Bill and I grew complacent, and didn't acknowledge the warning. Then Lolly would shout again, much louder, "Car behind!" We had heard it the first time, of course, and it was as confusing to hear it a second time as it was annoying for Lolly not to know if we *had* originally heard it. So the question of clearly acknowledging warnings caused the first disharmony on the trip. Lolly got miffed.

"How do I know if you hear me?" she complained. Then she rode in silence for several hours just to drive the point home. We really couldn't see behind us reliably from the forward positions and that afternoon, after independently reaching the conclusion that Lolly had good reason to be upset, we talked it out. From then on the warning was always acknowledged. "Car behind!" "Okay." "Okay." Our safety net was restored and Lolly was happy again. Her warnings were so faithful and timely that Bill and I relied heavily upon them.

"You guys do the leading, and I'll do the warning," she said.

It was a good trade-off, because Bill and I were stronger and were better able to lead in the headwinds we were experiencing. Having the rear guard duty, Lolly felt that her contribution offset not taking a turn at leading. It was a system that not only worked well, but Lolly's vigilance proved invaluable. I don't think she missed reporting a vehicle on the whole trip.

If you've ever been in one of those mountain lodges that are constructed of logs and nestled in the timber as though Daniel Boone himself had carved them out with an axe, then you know what the Lochsa Lodge was like. Inside you would expect to see moose antlers and maybe a bear hide tacked up beside an old pair of snowshoes on a log wall darkened by time and smoke. We weren't disappointed. In fact, we were delighted because it had been a long morning and we were growing resigned to peanut butter and jelly sandwiches again. Evidently the sign warning of no services didn't count the Lochsa Lodge, but we sure did.

It was warm inside, and we took off our protective gear and soaked up heat from the wood stove. We were in an outer dining room with high ceilings, the load-bearing logs of the open, soaring roof structure clearly visible. Old mounts of elk, deer and goat looked down at us with glassy eyes. The wood floors and heavy, handmade wooden furniture completed the cozy atmosphere. We found we were sharing with one other couple, who were on their way to Bethel, Alaska, after wintering in Albuquerque.

A woman—fiftyish, pleasant—came out to take our order. "What would you like?"

"We'll try those jumbo hamburgers." The other couple had been eating them, and they looked delicious.

They were delicious. So were the huge sweet rolls we had afterwards. The woman waited on two Forest Service types, and then came over to our table.

"Have you been in this country long?" I asked.

She smiled. "I was raised along this river. I've been away for awhile, been in forty-eight of the fifty states. Now, I spend most of my time right here. Running the lodge keeps us pretty busy."

We learned she was one of the owners, and heard how she and her husband had purchased the lodge only a couple of years ago, and now were in all kinds of trouble. The lodge was located on land leased from the Forest Service, and the sale involved the transfer of the lease. Allegedly, the previous owners wanted to renege on the sale now that the new ones had built up the business, and the matter was in litigation. As we sat in that cozy and homey lodge building, such matters seemed incongruous. Yet the owners were undeniably concerned.

Wanting to change the subject, I commented on the bear mount.

"We killed a bear near here recently," she said. "There are lots of them around."

After all, we were right on the edge of the wilderness. And the previous night, we had camped on an old river bar. A marshy spot nearby was obviously a bear feeding area, and I was apprehensive about pitching our tents near there. But a check for tracks or sign turned up no evidence of recent usage, so we camped and slept lightly. In the morning, our tent flies were solid with frost.

Near Lochsa Lodge we passed two young men hiking east with backpacks. I slowed with the intention of stopping to talk, and then thought better of it. We were covering ground quickly compared with walking speed, and the two might resent the comparative ease with which the bikes carried our loads. So I went around them and kept on going. It wasn't until we returned from the trip that we learned they were from Ashland, as we were, and were heading for New York.

We had read about Lolo Pass, a scourge on the bike route because of a 6-mile climb at six-percent grade. It leads the highway east from the Clearwater drainage, over the Bitterroot range and into Montana. We were ready for it, but the weather wasn't going to cooperate. It grew cloudy and colder, and rained occasionally. We were down in the low gears, pulling up that hill. We could see a storm cell coming, and we wanted to get over the top before it hit. It was a tie.

Knowing we would get cold coasting down the other side, we put on all our protective gear at the top, and took photos at the summit sign. A short distance beyond, we stopped at a "Welcome to Montana" sign and took more photos in a snowstorm. Then we began a wet, slippery and cold descent, blinking constantly because of snowflakes that blew in behind our glasses. Finally the snow stopped and a few miles after that, the road was dry.

How would you feel, riding along at 20 miles an hour, if suddenly a five-pound object hurtled past your head? Vulnerable, that's the way I felt. Bill and Lolly just laughed. The fact that the object was a chicken would not have lessened the damage. When I swerved out to pass the birds, which were on the right shoulder of the road, I had no idea they would become airborne and set up a pursuit curve that led right in front of my nose. You see some strange things while bicycling, I thought. And I also made a mental note to pay more attention to chickens; they might be airworthy.

Lolo, Montana, has no motel, so we had to ride on into Missoula, an 11-mile addition to what had already been an exhausting day. The route we were riding was the one favored by Bikecentennial, the bicycle travel association, and wouldn't you know, their headquarters are in Missoula. We had joined Bikecentennial and were using their maps. But I must confess, looking at a map of the United States, one can't help but wonder why the route takes a long swing northwards to Missoula, and then another swing southward, which altogether adds several hundred miles to the trip. But now that we were in Missoula, we weren't going to miss out on our visit to the headquarters.

Next morning found us riding in downtown Missoula, trying to find Bikecentennial headquarters. This was the largest town we had been in since the start, and we had to deal with traffic lights and congestion everywhere. Finally we found the building.

Some nice photos hung on the wall inside, of many different people on many different kinds of bikes. I signed the log book on the counter and checked to see what other cyclists had logged in recently. Lolly and Bill also signed. The people behind the counter were looking at us as if to ask, "What do you think you're doing here?" so I asked them what the purpose and objective of the association were. There was some stuttering around, and then a lot of smooth words that had no substance. The bunch of little office cubicles appeared ridiculous, I suppose because we were accustomed to being in the open. We felt very out of place, and soon left. Riding back to the laundromat where our clothing was drying, we felt a real letdown. Visiting the headquarters had been a high point in our expectations for days, and it had been an anticlimax, almost unfriendly.

The only thing you could imagine nicer than riding up through the Bitterroot Valley, where majestic snow caps guard the west and spring wildflowers in the fields stretch away to meet the timber dripping like dark icing from the canyons cutting the scarp, would be to do it on smooth roads. Something about the way Montana blacktop—a cold mix, perhaps—is laid down on secondary roads defies the smoothing of the roller; while doubtless providing good traction for autos, the surface drums at high-pressure bike tires with a constant, less-than-gentle vibration. The shoulders, which we rode when provided, were no smoother.

We had picked up mail at Lolo, our first mail stop on the trip, and besides going through the letters like kids through Christmas presents, we were happy to get a package of energy bars from our daughter Cindy. We snacked on these as we made progress through Stevensville, Corvallis and Hamilton.

The pancakes at Karen's Cafe in Darby, eastward as they were of those we had previously consumed, were indeed larger. But we weren't having any trouble eating the helpings, and some mornings we would order an extra one or two. This morning two men, one in his sixties and the other younger, were sitting at an adjoining table.

"Where are you headed?" the younger man asked.

It was the inevitable question, one we had come to expect. We told him.

"I do some bike riding," he confided. "My friend here is starting to ride too."

"I want to get my wife enthused about riding," the older man lamented, "but she thinks she's too old, or that it's not something women do."

Lolly responded quickly. "I'll bet she'd like it."

"She probably would, if I could just get her started. I wish she could meet you."

From the younger man we gleaned some information about the 7,000-foot pass ahead of us, paid the bill and walked out to the bikes. Last night, in our tents in a huge campground where we had been the only patrons, it had been cold. This day was no warmer, and we had to put on all of our cold-weather gear again.

It v̇ 's just past the middle of May, a changeable time and rushing the season a bit in the high mountains. Aside from a few days when temperatures had almost reached the sixties, we had been bundled up against cold and wind chill all the time. Only when climbing passes generated enough body heat could we strip down to shorts and jerseys. Sometimes, especially going downhill on east or north slopes, we got so cold that our hands and feet ached, even though we had on wind-shell gloves and shoe covers. Were we too early, we wondered out loud? It didn't do any good to talk about that now. We were two weeks on the road, and Lolly's electronic odometer flashed the message that we were 1,100 miles into the ride.

"Car!" Lolly shouted.

We didn't worry much until we heard the vehicle slowing down as it came up behind. We identified a pickup with Montana plates . . . and then the vehicle was passing us, slowing more. As the truck swerved back into the lane directly in front of us and slowed to match our speed, I saw there were two men in it. The passenger turned in his seat, facing back towards us, and raised something black in his hand. With a quick jolt of adrenaline I realized the man might have a weapon. I started to shout.

"It's the two from the cafe," Lolly said. "He's got a camera."

Sure enough, I could see the camera now, and the older man was using it. He took a couple of pictures, waved, and then the pickup was accelerating. I felt foolish at my reaction, but that didn't stop my hands from shaking. A little riding would work off the adrenaline. The man had his photos; I hope his wife was inspired by three bicyclists, with maybe a little grey hair showing beneath their helmets, bundled up against the cold, bumping along the road that follows the Bitterroot River.

# 6 MONTANA

### DARBY, MONTANA—TWIN BRIDGES, MONTANA

When you visualize something like a long bike trip from the warmth, comfort and security of more normal routines, it is easy to get carried away with the romance of it all. My mind conjures up scenes of lush, green valleys, a sparkling stream paralleling the road, and perhaps rail fences. In the near distance are timbered slopes with snow caps for a backdrop. In this vision it is warm, but not too warm, the road is smooth and there are no bugs. There is also no traffic. In your mind's eye you ride endlessly through countryside of great beauty, seeing unique, exciting things and meeting unusual people. No hazards appear, at least none that you can't imagine your equipment and abilities coping with easily.

You never imagine the lung-searing climbs up steep grades that seem certain to burst your chest if your leg muscles don't play out first. And you certainly never imagine being overtaken on a two-lane road by a huge truck that, as it passes you, is in turn meeting another truck going the opposite direction, the three of you at a given point on the same road at the same time, and there is no shoulder—nothing but a jagged, pavement-edge drop-off of half a foot into the gravel.

Does half a century of living cause one to perceive these things differently from what would have been the case at, say, twenty? I don't think so. The dreams of adventure are no different, in my opinion, and surely one's visualization is no more optimistic or realistic regardless of one's age. My reaction to danger has always been about the same. I tend to see potentials more readily than others do, and consequently I try to avoid some of the hazards that might sneak up and catch me unaware. But my awareness of potentials does not seem to overpower or taint the romanticism of my dreams. I love to think about adventures to come even though I fully appreciate the truth of the old saying that "anticipation is better than realization."

Realization was setting in. For one thing, the distance we had to cover

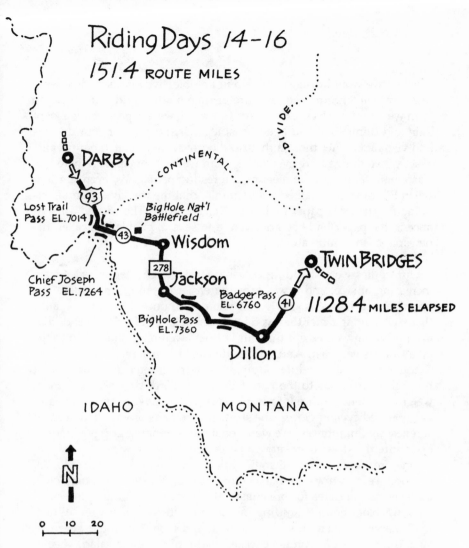

# Riding Days 14-16
## 151.4 ROUTE MILES

DARBY

93

Lost Trail
Pass EL.7014

CONTINENTAL

DIVIDE

Big Hole Nat'l
Battlefield

43

Wisdom

278

Chief Joseph
Pass EL.7264

Jackson

Badger Pass
EL. 6760

TWIN BRIDGES

41

1128.4 MILES ELAPSED

Big Hole Pass
EL.7360

Dillon

IDAHO

MONTANA

N

0   10   20

and the time we had to cover it in were becoming clear to us. Lolly's little red dots on the map, marking the theoretical end of each day, had taken on new meaning. At the end of every day we would record the distance actually covered, and we were overjoyed when it was greater than our planned mileage. If it was less, we would rationalize that we would make it up the next day. I was the one who was pushing. If we stopped too long anywhere, or if we hadn't made our mileage, I would keep pressure on to get back in the saddle and go at it again. The math was so simple—we had a certain number of miles to cover, and if we intended that Bill make the ride all the way across, we had a limited number of days to make it in. I think Lolly and Bill resented my keeping to the schedule because I was persistent at it.

When we would discuss the trip in an objective manner, there were few complaints. Sure, the pressure of time made us ride longer hours than we otherwise would have. And sure, we were experiencing a lot of pain and things that had been conspicuously absent from our dreams and visualizing. Yet though the trip did not seem to match our dreams exactly, two things were even better than we had anticipated: there was excitement, and we were meeting interesting people. We even learned, when Bill called and talked with Connie, that the weekly column I was doing for the local paper had been well received. The second appearance in the paper had been delayed, and several people had called the newspaper to inquire about it.

Our bodies were shedding excess poundage. Our leg muscles were increasing in size, and it was growing easier to pump up grades. The improvement happens slowly and you don't notice it until you realize that you're going faster than you had been able to before. All conditioning was going well except that our bottoms weren't getting used to the bike saddles very fast. And our hands were often sore.

You lean forward while riding, transferring some of your weight through your hands to the handlebars. The sorer your seat, the more weight you tend to throw forward onto your hands. Even with space-age, padded cycling gloves, the stress on the pads of your palm causes soreness and numbness. We were constantly changing grip positions to distribute the stress over various parts of our hands.

One great bonus was the ability to eat anything we wanted. Most of the food we craved was high in carbohydrates. We were now completely addicted to pancakes for breakfast. We were able to locate good salad bars like bloodhounds sniffing out a trail, whether they were in fast-food places or restaurants. When we found them we would gorge on such things as fruit, cottage cheese, macaroni or potato salad, vegetables and breads. Oddly, we had little appetite for fried foods or heavy meat dishes. Other patrons in restaurants would stare aghast at the huge helpings, and look incredulous as we went back for seconds. We were burning thousands of calories each day, and some of the lunches and dinners we put away would have been obscene in any other context.

Sleeping became simple. As soon as we turned in we dropped off to sleep. During the day, all that was necessary was to lean back or lie down for a few seconds, and we fell asleep instantly. We didn't get sleepy while riding, though; we were working too hard.

We had just crossed the Continental Divide on Lost Trail and Chief Joseph Passes, over 7,200 feet above sea level at the summit, when we saw a young man taking a bicycle from the top rack on his car.

"Hi," he said. "I'm going to coast down the mountain and then ride back up for the conditioning. This summer I go touring with a friend, and he's already training. He lives in high country in Colorado."

We learned that he was a mill accountant in Missoula for Champion National. Things had been slow at work, and this gave him time to do some riding and get into condition. We discussed the rumored closure at Champion National, but he was calm about it.

"If they close, I'll probably go on a long bike trip like you're doing."

Then he pulled on windproof gear and took off down the hill. We never did get his name but because each of us was on a bicycle, a sort of kinship was present. We watched him until he was out of sight before we turned and headed east.

Three feet of snow blanketed the timber on either side of the roadway, making us feel vulnerable and thankful that the plows had scraped down to bare pavement. We armored up against the afternoon chill on the shady side of the mountain, and began our descent.

Historical markers in this area commemorate two subjects: the Lewis and Clark exploration, and dates and happenings of the Nez Perce war. On the alluvial plain to the east of the mountains, we came to Big Hole National Battleground, where a large visitor's center has been built to house exhibits and publicize the spot where a comparative handful of Nez Perce warriors defeated the U.S. Seventh Cavalry.

Usually, such exhibits and hoopla, with their accompanying slide shows and fifth-grade approach, leave me cold. This time it was different. We arrived after closing time, and so did not feel compelled to sit through the show or wander among the glass display cases of preserved relics. Instead, we took a self-guided tour pamphlet from the rack, walked around to the rear of the building out of the wind where it was warm and sunny, and picked out the landmarks of the battlefield. We took a few photos and then just sat in the sun. Gradually, I began to get the feel of the place, and to sense what had happened there long ago. It became easy to imagine the Nez Perce warriors, relentlessly pursued over hundreds of miles and fearful not only for their own lives but for their women and children as well, deciding to set up a massive ambush. Surely the astute among them realized it was a temporary victory that did not change the doom hanging over their way of life.

I could see tepee frames a mile or so away, on the grassy meadow down by the river. Evidently either re-enactments occurred here or else the Park Service wanted to create an authenticity for those who did not sit down and let the feeling of the spot seep into them. A small rodent— probably a prairie dog—partially emerged from its hole in the center of a mound of earth and watched us warily. As we got up to leave, it barked a sharp warning and dropped from sight. What had its ancestors seen on this spot?

We reached Wisdom, Montana, by riding across long stretches of gray-green sagebrush. An occasional antelope would dash madly away in alarm if it had wandered too close to the road, only to stop a few yards further out to stare in curiosity. On two occasions, far out on the flat where bright green carpets of spring grass colored the twisting, shallow watercourses, we spotted dancing pairs of sandhill cranes.

There are 120 people in Wisdom, at least according to the sign, and the town had all the markings of being a gathering center for a very large, if sparsely populated, area. Three motels and two cafes were open as we rode in. A hearse drove slowly out of town, but we didn't think much about it. The Nez Perce Motel got our vote, which seemed only fair after our recent battleground visit. We checked in and then rode back to Letty's Cafe, which we knew would be in the middle of a typical, small-town Saturday night.

It wasn't.

The cafe was separated from the bar section, where two or three men were sitting quietly, by a short wall and a few posts. We could see one other couple in the cafe. No one was saying much, and that's not like any Saturday night I had experienced. Except Letty, and Letty clearly had a lot to say to everyone. From the humor in her voice she obviously delighted in life, and could—and would—say whatever she wanted to whomever she wanted to say it.

Letty walked with a pronounced limp. Watching her made you think not only that it must hurt her to move, but also that a little hurt wasn't going to stop her. She handed us menus with a big smile.

"It's a little quiet around town tonight," she said, "The bartender's ninety-six-year-old father just died of a stroke."

She didn't have to add that in a small town where everyone knew everyone else, this was a blow to all. Then she brightened.

"My fried chicken is the best."

"Okay. We need lots of water, too."

Letty brought a pitcher full. By the time the chicken was ready, we began to hear some conversation coming from the bar. A local woman came into the cafe and engaged in some lively banter with Letty before they agreed on some point involving an obscure happening in Wisdom. Then an older couple, travellers by their dress, came in and sat down. Letty went over to serve them while her husband traded back and forth between bartending and helping in the kitchen. We could see out the front window to where a few locals were arriving at the bar across the street. Soon, a game of horseshoes had developed at one of the several pits beside the road. It was evident the shock was wearing off.

"Where are you from?" The older couple were both smiling at us.

"Ashland, Oregon," Lolly said.

"I've chained up my rig many times at the foot of your Siskiyou Mountains," the man said. "I'm Fred Anderson, and this is my wife. I'm retired now, we live north of here. I used to drive long-haul trucks. Yessir, those Siskiyous are something!"

"Where are you headed?" Mrs. Anderson asked.

"We're headed for Virginia Beach, Virginia," Lolly replied.

I watched Letty smile at that. She had not missed the "Coast to Coast" jerseys we had on.

"Wow!" Fred Anderson exclaimed. "That's a long way." He thought a minute. "But you've made a good start on it already."

More people came into the cafe, and now livelier talk issued from the bar. We worked slowly at the chicken, listening to the conversations around us.

"Hi, Letty, have you heard about —" And Letty either had, or hadn't. We enjoyed sitting and watching, feeling the town come to life. Two horseshoe pits were occupied now, and people were standing around watching.

"I think I'll have some ice cream," Bill said.

Without guilt we all ordered some, knowing that the work we were doing was responsible for our atrocious appetites and that we would burn off the calories. Besides, it gave us a chance to stay in the cafe where it was warm and where the booths were padded and soft. Each new arrival in the cafe would stare at us as if we were from a different planet.

A couple, dressed like the tourists they were, came into the cafe.

"We're almost out of gas," the man said to Letty. "And the gas station is closed."

Letty's husband made a quick phone call, then turned to the couple.

"The man from the station is on his way down to get your gas," he said.

"Thanks."

Then the couple looked embarrassed, as if they didn't know what to do. They sat down in a booth and ordered coffee.

We paid the bill on the way out.

"I'm open at six," Letty offered.

"Have any pancakes?"

"The best you've ever eaten!"

The observers at the horseshoe games across the street decided we were more interesting, and watched us walk the length of the block. A large English sheepdog, his coat trimmed shorter than necessary even for summer, came up to us, wiggling every bit of his huge body in an irresistible bid for attention.

Two men climbed out of an old, beat-up Plymouth station wagon with Pennsylvania plates and walked toward us. They were not bearded, they were just plain unshaven and looked as if they had been on the road a long time.

"Want to buy a typewriter?" the shorter of the two asked. "We need gas money to get out of town."

He offered an ancient manual portable that definitely had seen better days; a couple of keys were missing.

"No thanks. But maybe somebody around here will."

I doubted it, though. Wisdom probably had some way of dealing with such shady-looking characters, but I didn't have the slightest idea what it would be. Saturday night or not, and much as we would have liked to learn the ending of the typewriter-vending episode, we rode to our motel, wheeled the bikes inside and turned in. We had plenty of riding ahead of us.

The southward slope of the Big Hole River valley and the light tailwind made easy riding. Having a tailwind was almost a curiosity for us; we'd had only a few and always longed for that gentle push of air at our backs. Letty's pancakes, as big as her heart was, were wearing off nonetheless when we got to Jackson.

Imagine a log building huge enough to house an Olympic-size pool in one end, rooms upstairs, and a dance hall, bar and restaurant on the down floor and you have the Jackson Hot Springs Lodge. We stopped and went in because the huge log structure and the log guest cabins surrounding it looked strange sitting there on the flat land. But by all indications this had been a lively place in years past when hot springs were more of a craze and people often journeyed to them for health reasons. The interior had lots of charm, with exposed, natural logs, planked floors, high ceilings and an almost overwhelming spaciousness. Around the pool it was damp and steamy, with an odor suggesting dry rot. We learned that the hot springs were too warm for pool use, so the water was used first to heat the buildings. Even the brass foot rail in the bar had hot water circulating through it. We looked at the collections of guns, arrowheads, big-game trophies and even shoulder patches and World War II medals before we went across the street to Rose's.

Rose's was primarily a bar, but it was the only place in Jackson where it looked like we might get something to eat on this Sunday morning.

Andy, around thirty-five and with a bushy, black beard, was the bartender in Rose's. We had seen the small sign advertising the bakery goods Andy made when not busy tending the bar. This morning only one man sat at the bar, and Andy gave us his full attention, dragging up the only table and chairs.

"Do you do the baking?" I asked.

Andy nodded proudly. All of a sudden it was plain that his baking was more important to him than tending bar. We looked over the menu, but couldn't keep our eyes off an apple pie that seemed ready to burst with juicy filling.

"I'll have the pie," I said, "and a scoop of ice cream on top."

Bill hesitated, as if he felt guilty at the thought of having dessert for lunch, but in another minute we had all ordered the pie. Andy served it with a smile and then waited, as if our reaction to his pie were of the utmost importance. He needn't have worried; the pie was the kind your mother makes.

"Wayne here," offered Andy, indicating the lone fellow at the bar, "has his first day off since October."

"That's right," Wayne affirmed. "Been feeding on the ranch all winter."

He didn't indicate if it was his ranch, or if he was working for someone else. We looked at him more closely, at his wide-brimmed hat, the heavy canvas coat he wore even indoors, his faded blue jeans and the rough-out leather riding boots. Nothing for show here—this man dressed this way all the time because it was the functional way for him.

"Do you often feed with teams in this valley?" I asked. We had seen cattle being fed hay from a horse-drawn wagon a few miles back.

"Yes," Wayne answered. "That way you can let the team keep moving while you go back and throw off bales. You can't do that safely with a tractor. A man can feed by himself using a team."

"What are those long poles and racks up in the valley for?" Lolly asked.

Wayne laughed. "Those are derricks for stacking hay. A crew using two derricks and four or five buck rakes can stack two hundred tons a day."

We learned more about ranching practices in the area from Wayne, who was no less curious about our undertaking. We told him about the ride, and briefly described some of our experiences. Wayne wouldn't have been cast in any western movie roles; he was too authentic for that. If we had lived in that valley, we would have found close friends in Andy and Wayne, I'm sure. When we left, Andy was beaming, and at our request trotted out three of the biggest apple fritters we had ever seen so we could take them along. They must have weighed two pounds apiece.

The pavement was going by in a blur. Coasting at high speed on a bicycle is always scary, and it's hard to keep your mind off thoughts like "What if the front wheel comes off?" The roughness of the road now was minimized as my bike floated over the smaller variations in the pavement. I didn't take my eyes off the "track" the bike wheels were following, a route selected and changed constantly as I flew downhill, ever alert for chuckholes or debris. We still had a tailwind that afternoon.

Then Bill sailed by me; he had been drafting and constantly picking up speed as I broke the wind ahead of him. I let him go and found the wake in the air made by his passing. Now that he was in front providing the windbreak, I began accelerating until I had to pull out and pass him. This slingshot process would repeat itself. We had become accustomed to this phenomenon, and enjoyed going downhill in this fashion when we were certain there was no other traffic. Lolly would usually coast along behind, I suspect using her brakes just enough to keep her speed even. This afternoon, because of the tailwind, we were going faster than ever before. When the road levelled out at the bottom, I let the bike coast to a stop.

"Wow!" Lolly said. "We were going forty-two miles an hour!"

That was the fastest we had gone while coasting, and it was thrilling—besides being scary. A crash at such a speed would have had serious consequences.

We ate our giant apple fritters then. No matter how large such portions might have seemed to us in the past, it was clear to us while we were riding that food was fuel. We craved certain foods above all others, besides our beloved salad-bar fare. When available, sweet rolls or doughnuts were always irresistible. We also ate maple bars and other baked items that, in our normal routine at home, we would have passed up. It isn't easy to carry bakery items on a bike to use as in-between snacks because they crush easily and are heavy in any quantity. If we could reach a cafe around lunch time, we would eat there. Many times, in order to reach a town or settlement where we could get something to eat, we would delay lunch. When we did this, if we went for very long before we finally ate, our strength seemed to diminish rapidly.

Peanut butter and jelly sandwiches for lunch were standard fare when we weren't near a town. Much of the time we had a loaf of whole wheat bread, a jar of peanut butter and a jar of jelly or jam inside a plastic bag, lashed onto the rear of our bikes with bungee cord. We also carried bananas and oranges, which are heavy but provide a lot of energy. Lolly and Bill might have laughed at my habit of taking the peel off an orange in one piece, but they ate the slices gratefully.

For snacks we relied on various forms of granola and energy bars. It was plain after just a few days of riding that some of these bars provided real energy boosts, while others left us as hungry and lethargic as if we hadn't eaten anything. As soon as we discovered the "good" kinds, we would look for them every time we went into a grocery for shopping. It became a real accomplishment each time we were able to find some good granola bars, and we would stock up. One time I had over thirty of them in my pack.

We always kept at least two freeze-dried dinners in reserve for the times we camped and weren't near any cafes. At these times we had instant oatmeal and Tang for breakfast.

Our steady weight loss didn't bother me at the time because I thought we were still overweight and the situation would eventually balance input and output.

Headwinds were strong that afternoon. We stopped for a rest and snack right beside the road, in a little hollow with a cut bank that offered some protection from the wind. Parked in the hollow fifty yards away was a bright yellow D-4 Caterpillar. We were admiring the machine as we ate when suddenly two men and a woman appeared from the opposite side of the road, where we knew there was a ranch.

The rancher approached with angry strides and at first we thought he must be coming to throw us out of our resting place. We didn't see how we were hurting anything, but we readied ourselves for whatever was going to happen. Instead of coming to us, the man jumped on the D-4 and fired it up. With the stack belching black smoke at full throttle, the dozer clattered up to the roadside in a cloud of dust. The driver stopped barely long enough for the other two, whom we took to be his wife and son, to lay some old tires under the cleats when he roared forward again, then stopped because there weren't tires enough to cushion the pavement all the way across the highway. Son and wife were running madly back and forth, taking tires from behind and laying them in front of the tracks. They had barely finished when the rancher let out the clutch and the dozer jumped forward and off the roadway, the tracks clacking in a protest you could hear for a mile.

The rancher jolted towards the house and then spun the dozer into a fenced area that appeared to be a garden plot. In the middle of the garden was a large pile of manure, beside which was parked a huge rubber-tired loader, much bigger than the D-4. The man jumped off the dozer and onto the loader, and began trying to spread the manure out over the quarter-acre plot. His wife and son just watched as the diesel snarled and protested the high-gear work with lots of black smoke.

Apparently the loader wasn't doing what he wanted, because the rancher jumped back onto the dozer, in a very agitated manner, and attacked the manure pile. We watched incredulously as the D-4 sped back and forth, every maneuver evidencing the displeasure of the driver.

"What do you think that's all about?" Bill said finally.

"It looks to me like the woman wants her garden area tilled, and the husband doesn't want to do it." I was speculating, but that would explain the stances we were observing.

"Yes," Lolly said, nodding. "That's what it looks like to me, too."

We put away the wrappers from the energy bars, "good" ones, and picked up the bikes. As we rode away, the dozer was still moving back and forth like an angry, yellow beetle. We were far down the road before the clatter of the tracks faded from our hearing.

Well, I thought, at least we get along well with each other, not at all like the scene we've just witnessed. We had long ago discussed the possibility that our enforced togetherness could cause irritation. But each of us had made flexible sacrifices to the needs of the group. Lolly had been upset when we didn't acknowledge her traffic warnings, but her expectation had been reasonable. So far, all in all, we three were doing well as a harmonious group. We had been riding every day for sixteen days, and our routines were getting pretty smooth. All the same, the rancher's performance that afternoon had been impressive. I made a mental note: if Lolly wanted the garden prepared, I would do it willingly and not attack it with a bulldozer.

*May 19–20*

# 7

# COLDER

We felt good when we reached Dillon, mostly because of the 17 miles of downhill riding with the wind at our backs that had just brought us into town. The route took us right by Western Montana College.

"I think they've played against our women's volleyball team at SOSC in Ashland," Lolly said, having identified the gym.

We took time out to admire the striking architecture and brick construction of the campus. Beautiful grounds complement the structures, which have a style that seemed to us almost European and not at all what you would expect to see in Dillon, Montana. We took some photos before looking for a motel.

When the first motel we investigated didn't look good to her, Lolly suggested, "Why don't we camp?"

I agreed. "Fine with me."

Bill nodded. We had intended to camp a great deal of the time, but the cold weather in the mountains had us stopping at motels often. Feeling tired was a factor too, I'm sure; it takes energy to set up a camp. But this afternoon the weather had warmed a little, and the tailwind had let us finish the day with energy to spare.

A road sign and a system of arrows directed us to a campground at the edge of town. We were pleased to find it clean, and as the breeze was still blowing, overjoyed to find windbreak fences around each of the tent sites that effectively blocked it. We were stopping early; by 5:30 we had the tents up and were at the Crossroads Restaurant extravagantly enjoying the prime rib. Oh, well, I thought, this makes up for those freeze-dried dinners.

A couple came over to the table, smiling as if meeting old friends. I didn't recognize them.

"Hi," the woman said. "We passed you on the road near Jackson!"

I guess we did stand out; no one else in the restaurant was wearing riding shorts and jerseys, or encumbered with helmets. We chatted

# Riding Days 16-17    *May 19–20*
## 121.8 ROUTE MILES

awhile and I wondered at the camaraderie that had developed just because the couple had passed us on the road. Were these two of the people we had talked about before we decided to make the ride? People who wanted to do something adventurous but never quite got around to it? We had seen envy in many people we encountered on the trip, and a desire to experience what the ride was like through talking to us. A few such conversations left me feeling very negative. These people, though, were warm and sincere, and I felt good after we parted.

Lolly and Bill used the laundromat while I talked with a man who was camped by himself in a large fifth-wheel trailer. He was an extension agent from Grant County, Washington.

"I have friends who run a big sheep operation east of here," he told me. "I've been up there all day. Lots of antelope on the place, and red foxes. I'm surprised at how many red foxes there are."

We talked about the Montana country, and I could tell he loved the huge expanses of rangeland and the mountains in the same way I do.

"There's everything up on that ranch," he said admiringly. "All kinds of wildlife. And they're doing all right with the place, too."

The tailwind continued next morning, and it grew warmer. For the first time since we started we were able to ride without our long johns. We rode on at 20 miles an hour to Twin Bridges before rewarding ourselves with an ice cream sandwich. The road changed direction here, and again we were faced with a headwind. We didn't realize it at the time, but the road's change of direction marked the real beginning of our battle with the winds.

We rode through Nevada City, a relic of a mining town made up of some authentic ruins of cabins, homes and sod shanties. Looking just too perfect, on the east side of the road, was a group of buildings that exactly fit the era. They were authentic too, but many of them had been moved onto the site from other locations. The resulting late-1800's town has unquestionable charm, and the restoration and reconstruction have been faithfully accomplished. But to my eye, knowing how it came to be gave it an artificial and phony look. On to Virginia City.

Here the authentic buildings were in use and some had been restored. Little in the way of gold mining goes on today in Virginia City. The mining is all for the ore in tourists' pocketbooks. We locked up the bikes and wandered the streets, enjoying the careful copies of early businesses being run by the local merchants. We had three scoops of ice cream apiece in the parlor, then looked into the candy shop across the street. We were astounded at one of the largest inventories of hard candies we'd ever seen.

At the newspaper shop, which specialized in novelty printing, a young man was striking single copies of a Virginia City news sheet that proclaimed in huge black type: "CANCAN GIRL ARRESTED! MEG SMITH IN JAIL!" Meg Smith, from New York judging by her accent, stood by the counter inspecting the proof copy. She looked fifty-ish and overweight. "I'll take two dozen," she said.

A couple riding a huge Honda motorcycle with South Carolina plates, a vehicle with built-in luggage containers and double seats, rode up across the street, parked and began sightseeing. They were both dressed in conspicuous western style. They might get by riding that motor in those boots, I thought, but I'd like to see them try a bicycle.

Somehow, just after we left town headed south, a 7,000-foot pass sneaked in. We were veterans of higher passes than that, but not in the kind of headwind that now faced us. It was tough riding because the wind was gusty. A sharp gust would bring us almost to a complete stop. We were in lowest gear on this hill, really hurting, when a purring motor sound from behind warned of the approach of the couple on the Honda. They went by effortlessly at 60 miles an hour, stereo blaring, waving at us. We could see their faces inside the plastic bubble helmets, and they were obviously having fun. For a minute resentment welled up, then subsided as we resignedly ground up the hill. *We* were the ones who had decided to cross the country under our own power.

Scully's Motel attracted us because it was set back from the main street on a gravel drive. Not that there was much traffic in Ennis, or on the secondary roads we had been travelling, but the place appeared friendly and quiet.

I walked into the office home of the owners, where an older couple sat in their kitchen. I was about to ask about a room when the man jumped up.

"Darn!" he said, picking up a slingshot and running out the door.

As I watched, he drew back the weapon and let fly. A half dozen blackbirds took wing and disappeared behind the buildings as the man came back.

"Those darned blackbirds keep the pine siskins and lazuli buntings away from our bird feeder," he complained. "I shoot at 'em all the time, but they come back after a little while."

"Ever hit one?" I asked.

"Once in a while." He looked pleased.

The wife took care of renting the rooms, that was clear from the way she looked at me. She stared out at Lolly and Bill standing by the bikes and hesitated; then she rented us the room. I paid her and started to leave.

"You're not going to take those bikes into the room, are you?" she asked.

"We always do," I said. "We'll be careful."

"I don't want you to drip oil on the carpet, or anything."

I assured the woman that we weren't going to drip oil on the carpet and would, in fact, take extra care in the room. She didn't seem satisfied, but she said no more.

Later, we were sitting in Betti's Cafe just a short way down the street, having dinner. A local cowboy was eating with a neighbor in the booth just across from us.

"Yep," he said, "those bears been in the garbage can every night!"

I could feel Lolly's ears perk up. Probably because bears are bigger than people and have claws and teeth, Lolly has an unreasoning fear of them. I hoped the cowboy wouldn't stay on the subject.

"One of them's a big one," he went on. "Seen him several times this past month."

"There's lots more bears around than there used to be," the neighbor offered.

And then they launched into a bear story about a marauding bear and dogs and men that ended with wounded dogs and a dead bear. Great, I thought, now we won't get Lolly to agree to camp within a hundred miles of here. A glance at her confirmed this. Then the cowboys changed the subject, and we began to relax as we sat listening to the talk around us. We learned that the unusual-looking horses we had seen as we rode into Ennis were Norwegian Dunns, a short, stocky breed developed for work in mines in Norway. We were accepted quickly into the group conversation, and were soon telling about our ride. When we left the cafe, however, I knew that for a while camping was out.

"Let's stay in motels until we get out of the mountains," Lolly said as we were riding back to the motel. It sounded more like a statement than a question.

In the morning Lolly took a pound of brown sugar over to the woman at the office. We had only been able to buy a two-pound bag, which was too heavy, so we decided to give half of it to the owner. Now the woman was all smiles. I wondered if she had checked the room while we were gone to see if we had dripped oil on the carpet. For whatever reason, her reaction to the gift of sugar was warm and friendly.

As we rode through the valley leading south from Ennis, the winds were dead against us. Tufts of roadside grass waved sharply and creek-side willows swayed. The gods of headwinds were dancing merrily, mocking our feeble efforts to ride each mile.

A couple in a motor home passed us and waved.

"That's George and Shirley Shortridge," Lolly said.

We had talked to them in Betti's Cafe, and now the motor home turned off the road ahead at a fishermen's access point. We rode by, not very fast, matching our strength against the wind at a pace we hoped we could sustain. Off to one side we saw the motor home stop, and the retired couple got out with their fishing rods. Probably going to see if there are any brown trout under those grassy banks, I thought. And then the headwinds got all our attention for a while.

With the wind blowing hard, I forced my mind to think of other things as we ground along. Sometimes I would pick out a point along the road ahead, and concentrate on that until it fell behind. Or I would think about what lay ahead on the route. My idea was to focus on anything to avoid thinking about the continuous extra effort needed to keep the bikes moving against the headwind.

Try not to notice that your speed is 7 or 8 miles an hour on the level, when it should be nearly 20 with half the effort. Try not to notice that the wind shows no signs of letting up. And concentrate in drafting in a tight pace line. Bill used a small watch adhered to his handlebars as a means of timing our turns in the lead. We could always tell the strength of the wind by the unit of time between alternating leads. Lolly, our rear guard by mutual consent, continued her traffic watch.

Roads are not always smooth to bicycles, especially not on the shoulder where we tried to ride whenever possible. Their irregularities include all sorts of debris: rocks and gravel, pieces of tire, wire, v-belts, broken bolts, tire weights and nails, not to mention cracks, grooves and holes in the pavement itself. When you are riding you develop an automatic scanning sense that picks out a smooth route through the debris and rough spots. This is your track, and unconsciously it is being constantly adjusted by the requirements of balance and obstacle avoidance. The leading rider is often the only one who can see the track, and so is responsible for selecting a safe route for the bikes drafting behind. These riders cannot see the track and depend upon following the rear wheel of the bike ahead. We developed a system of calling out the hazards ahead. "Rock!" or "Rocks!" or "Hole!" were common exclamations, usually with one hand pointing at the hazard so the riders trailing behind would know its location.

At low speeds forced by headwinds or hills, obstacles were not difficult to deal with. Drafting at 20 miles an hour is an entirely different matter, and Bill and I had each had flats that were caused by hitting rocks or holes seen too late to avoid.

The Shortridges' motor home passed us again, bringing me out of the headwind-induced mesmerization. They waved as they went by, and for a minute the wake of their passing provided a windbreak. Then over the period of a few minutes the motor home became a receding dot in the distance and finally disappeared completely.

Every few miles we saw small herds of antelope in the fields beside the road, most of them either standing in hollows or draws to escape the wind, or lying down. I managed to get a picture of one herd before they scampered away only to stop once they had achieved their comfortable distance.

Something in the road ahead. Like a reverse replay of the motor home, it appeared as a tiny dot and slowly grew bigger and bigger as we approached. When we were within a mile there was no question; it was the Shortridges, and they were stopped.

Shirley was sitting inside, and as we wheeled around in front and stopped, she stepped down to the shoulder.

"George has gone to try to find a bigger jack," she said. "We couldn't raise it with ours."

The rear tire was completely flat, and there wasn't much space between the pavement and the axle. Bill looked at their small jack, and then he crawled under the motor home.

"I think I can get it under there," he said.

All I could do was encourage him. It took him about twenty minutes, twisting and shoving, but finally he had the jack under a solid lifting point.

"Give me the handle," Bill asked. Then he worked the handle for a few minutes. The cramped space was making it difficult. I took a turn at the jack, and before long we had the motor home up far enough to take the wheel off, and put on their spare. By the time George returned, we had the wheel changed. I could tell George was relieved. Their thanks was embarrassing.

"If you're ever in Vail—" George gave Lolly his card. Then they left.

We looked at the card. George was a retired pilot for a large corporation, it seemed, and now ran a ski school. We looked in the direction they had gone and watched the motor home disappear before we climbed on the bikes.

The road was blocked by a cattle drive of Black Angus, moving slowly in the same direction we were going. A pickup truck and a couple of horsemen moved slowly at the back of the herd, and we could see more riders up ahead.

I can't say we came upon the drive unawares. More than adequate evidence had splattered the pavement ever since the drive had come out onto the highway, forcing us to weave carefully to miss the fresh, green deposits.

The riders waved us ahead, while they cleared a way for us where the large black bodies were thickest. Then we were on our own. I thought, this should make a good picture, and stopped for a moment to use the camera. Of course, the cattle closed back together and I had to weave my way through to catch up with Lolly and Bill.

We were wary of the animals; these were range cattle, and some of the cows with calves looked like really mean critters. They would turn their heads slightly to keep an eye on us as we rode up behind, and we never knew if they would give way or decide to charge the three strange-looking apparitions on wheels trying to get through them. My attention was on the cattle, and I wasn't able to steer a clean route through the herd. Thank goodness for the fenders on the bikes!

We finally made it through the animals without serious incident, if you don't count having to clean off the bikes. One mean-eyed old cow in particular had wanted to take a swipe at me, but somehow our being on bikes worried her; I don't think she knew what we were. To avoid any chance of the herd catching up while we stopped for our snack, we rode on ahead a long way.

The wind was not letting up at all; if anything it was getting stronger. We were behind in our average for the day, and I wanted to try to make up the deficiency. Besides, we had reached the point where we wanted to get away from the sagebrush plains and into the land of forests and rivers we knew was ahead. Mostly, I guess, we were looking forward to riding in Yellowstone Park.

We were riding up the Madison River Valley, which was wide and gentle here, but that didn't disguise the fact that we were going upstream. As the afternoon wore on, so did our bottoms, and I found myself being unreasonably resentful of the headwinds. Each revolution of the pedal required not only physical effort, but—because of the ever-present temptation just to stop—mental toughness as well. After all, the only reason we weren't sailing along, having fun, was the fact that the wind was blowing straight from where we wanted to go. Maybe yesterday it blew the other way here, or it didn't blow at all, and maybe tomorrow it would be a tailwind if we waited. As we struggled for mile after mile, it became harder not to be angry at the wind.

The road had been traffic-free for more than an hour, so when a pickup truck headed the opposite direction slowed and stopped opposite us, Bill and I were wary. You can't tell what the intent of others might be, so we just naturally became watchful, getting ready for whatever might happen next. We stopped and took our feet out of the toe clips.

But the lone man in the pickup leaned out the window toward us, holding something wrapped in cellophane in his hand.

"Want some cookies?" he asked.

Surprised, Lolly took the bag he held out. The man smiled.

"Thanks," Lolly said, but the pickup truck was already moving.

Bill and I had been too surprised to even say thanks before the cookie man was off down the highway. We had expected something sinister and instead we got cookies. "Wilderness Cookies," the label proclaimed, listing a number of natural ingredients that were baked in Bozeman. We lost no time in trying them.

"He must be some sort of salesman for Wilderness Cookies," I said. "Probably on a route."

"Well, I don't believe it." Lolly said. "Here we are riding along the road, nearly exhausted, and a man stops and gives us a bag of cookies. Where else but on bicycles would that happen?"

"Maybe we looked like we needed them," Bill offered.

\* \* \*

Our goal was to reach West Yellowstone that day, and we still had a long way to go. It was hard to think positive thoughts as we rode. What if this headwind keeps up for days, I thought. Will we be able to complete the ride, especially in time for Bill to make it all the way across? Yesterday, when we had some downhill and a tailwind for a while, we only rode 68 miles. That isn't enough. Surely, when we get out of the mountains and onto the plains of Kansas, we'll have some of those 120-mile days we've read about, where a tailwind will push us across the flat country and make up for what we're suffering now. All our research had indicated that the prevailing winds crossing the country are from west to east, the direction we were riding. For days we had been heading south, but on turning eastward, we would have a tailwind. Yes, I told myself as we approached the end of the valley where the Madison exits from the mountains, we'll have favorable winds soon.

We stopped for a snack at a roadside store and cabins called Slide Inn, and met a couple from Evanston, Illinois. It was plain they were on vacation.

"Isn't this beautiful country?" The woman bubbled on.

"Yes, it is," Lolly said, but I knew what she was thinking. Wait until these Illinois folks see some really big mountains! The couple had hired a fishing guide and had one curled-up, dried-out trout of about two pounds, and they were bubbling with excitement from their experience "out West." Their enthusiasm was catching, and we certainly needed cheering up the way the ride had been going today. Soon we were laughing and talking about their trip and our ride as if we were old friends. We sat on a bench on the porch in front of the store, finishing our soft drinks.

The trees along the road beside Quake Lake and the Madison River provided shelter from the wind. Prior to 1959 no lake had existed here. In that year an earthquake moved a mountainside onto a campground beside the river, burying many people under earth and rock. The dammed river quickly formed Quake Lake, spilled over, and began the slow process of cutting away the obstruction. Undoubtedly, in a few thousand years, the river will do just that.

As we emerged from the canyon, we passed the dam forming Hebgen Lake, which was still frozen at the north end. We could see snowmobile tracks on the ice, made many weeks before. The wind, with no obstructions now, resumed blowing towards us as usual, colder from crossing the frigid lake. Clouds were piling up ahead, some of them towering thunderbangers.

Less than an hour of daylight remained as we turned onto the larger highway that led us along a corridor cut through the lodgepole pine forest towards West Yellowstone. It was only 7 miles now, but the wind was increasing rapidly, swaying the trees wildly. Papers, small sticks and aluminum beverage cans began flying by us, barely touching the ground and pavement. The cleared right-of-way for the highway formed a sort of tunnel through the trees that seemed to be concentrating the wind. We were being buffeted, making it difficult to ride.

We stopped to put on our rain gear as raindrops began to sting us. We were awed at the force of the wind, and had to ride very slowly and carefully. Lightning flashed to the south, followed by the crash of thunder two seconds later. Then more lightning. Suddenly we saw the trees on both sides of the road ahead bend alarmingly, shedding limbs, their tops nearly horizontal. I shouted a warning even though we could each see what was going to happen, and then the gust hit. Instantly, as if we had run into a wall, we were stopped and nearly knocked off the bikes before we could free our toe clips and brace ourselves. Luckily we were facing directly into the wind, or we wouldn't have been able to keep the bikes upright. As it was, we were busy keeping our balance while straddling the bikes. Somehow, although Bill had been blasted to a stop as Lolly and I had been, he managed to stay on the bike without putting his feet down. He gave me a smile at once both triumphant and grim.

Another monster gust flattened the trees, but we saw it coming in time and Lolly and I waited for it straddling our bikes. Bill continued his balancing act. And then the heavy rain hit. At least the rain heralded a relenting in the wind, and we were able to ride on into West Yellowstone.

The first motel we came to was closed. We rode on to the next, a well-known chain motel. I walked into the office in my rain gear and the woman behind the desk didn't even give me time to ask about a room.

"Our lowest-price rooms are forty dollars," she said, in a way that told me she thought that would stop us. "And that's for an upstairs single."

"Thanks," I said. Okay, lady, I thought, I saw you turn your nose up at the way we look. I didn't even care about the wet footprints on the office floor as I walked out.

"What's wrong?" Lolly asked me. You can't fool her very much.

"This place doesn't want us. Come on, we'll find a motel that does. This is May, and these places are empty as tombs."

Two blocks away we found a nice motel where the owner was not only glad to see us, but provided us with a suite. I wondered what the woman in the first motel had against bicyclists.

*May 21–24*

# 8

# DON'T CAMP
# IN THE PARK

"You're not going to camp in the park, are you?" The waitress in the Totem Cafe seemed aghast. "They don't want you to camp in the park because of the danger from bears. Last year a grizzly ate a camper just a little way down the road from here."

I took another bite of the excellent walleye steak dinner and glanced at Lolly. To get her to agree to camp in Yellowstone Park now would take some mighty tall convincing.

The three of us had been looking forward to riding through the park for some time. The beautiful scenery, the wildlife and the early season's unhurried pace would make it especially enjoyable, we thought. Now I knew Lolly would only be comfortable if we didn't try to camp in the park at all. As we went back to the warm motel room to write in our logs, I thought I would probably call West Thumb in the morning, after we talked to the ranger at the entrance. There should be rooms or cabins at West Thumb.

Next morning we rode expectantly up to the park entrance at West Yellowstone. We were feeling a real sense of accomplishment, having come this far, because Yellowstone National Park was a milestone in our ride, one of the biggies. Approaching that entrance was more thrilling than crossing the Rockies or reaching Missoula.

To the ranger on duty I outlined our route through the park and how we planned to leave by the south entrance.

"The pass is still closed," he said, shaking his head for emphasis. "It hasn't been opened yet because of snow. Another storm's due, and I don't know when it will be open."

"Are you sure?" My face must have registered shock. Not only had we

# Riding Days 18-21
## 270.4 ROUTE MILES

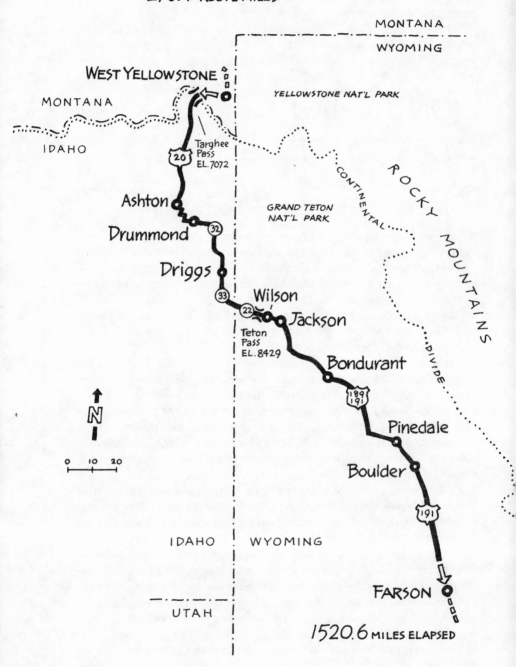

MONTANA
WYOMING

WEST YELLOWSTONE

MONTANA

IDAHO

YELLOWSTONE NAT'L PARK

20

Targhee
Pass
EL.7072

Ashton

Drummond

32

GRAND TETON
NAT'L PARK

CONTINENTAL

R O C K Y

Driggs

33

Wilson

22

Jackson

Teton
Pass
EL.8429

Bondurant

M O U N T A I N S

189
191

N

DIVIDE

Pinedale

0    10   20

Boulder

191

IDAHO    WYOMING

FARSON

UTAH

1520.6 MILES ELAPSED

been looking forward to riding through the park, but our route south-ward afterwards depended upon it.

"Yes, I'm sure. We usually have the roads open by this time, but there was so much snow last winter. I'm sorry." He looked distressed, and I realized our disappointment was showing clearly.

"Any suggestions?" I asked, oblivious to cars starting to pile up behind us. "Any detours that will take us around and lead us back to our route?"

"You could go out the east entrance and then turn south." The ranger did not seem bothered by the cars in the line. "That's through high desert country, mostly. Or you can go west into Idaho and back into Wyoming near Jackson."

I just stood there, stunned. The detours he was suggesting would add 100 miles to our route, maybe 200.

"I really am sorry," the ranger said.

We cleared the entrance lane, and the ranger waved to us. Then we backtracked a half mile to a tourist-information center we had passed. The woman inside gave us an Idaho map, since we had discarded ours when we reached Montana. The map showed the same alternatives the ranger had suggested.

"Well," I said, "it looks like we only have the two choices. Which one will it be?"

"I don't like the idea of riding hundreds of miles through the sage-brush in eastern Wyoming," Lolly said.

"At least in Idaho we would see some pretty country," Bill offered.

"The Idaho route looks a little shorter, too. Idaho it is, then," I said. "But I want to remind you that we rode all the way across Idaho a week ago."

Bill groaned and Lolly made a face. But off we pushed, back into Idaho—two steps back, toward the snow and the barroom in Drum-mond.

When I looked out from under the tent fly the next morning in that abandoned shed in Drummond, it was still snowing; the flakes were being driven horizontally. It had been a comfortable enough night in the tent, but the storm was more like winter than late May. Where was spring? We've had to take more than our share of weather, I thought. Is all this really necessary? Sure, we had envisioned adventure and thrills and challenges when we were home planning the trip. We had experi-enced thrills so far, like the exciting coast down off the backside of a steep pass, when the front wheel seems to drop out from under you, and the intense awareness of one's fragile body that always overwhelms me for a second or two when a semi-trailer passes, even when there is lots of room. It was also adventuresome to be out on the road, never knowing what lay before us each day or where we would be that night. Our moods changed with the way things were going, but I was especially pleased at the way I was able to react calmly to what the trip threw at us. Lolly, and Bill too, were showing a toughness that hadn't been at all visible during the planning stages. So, it seemed, the way tough adventurers react to a snowstorm is to press on.

Climbing out of the warm sleeping bag, I hollered at Bill to make sure he was awake, and then cooked breakfast in the shed while Lolly packed up inside the tent. Luckily the shed had been large enough for the bikes also, but even so we had placed plastic bags over the seats as usual to make sure they stayed dry.

The road back to the highway was treacherous with slushy snow on top of greasy, sticky clay. We couldn't ride in it, so we pushed the bikes up the hill until we came to the pavement, now snow-covered.

It was frightening, riding on the snowy road, especially since the strong crosswind was still blowing. Snow chilled the exposed side of our faces quickly, so we put on our balaklavas. Then the flakes got behind our riding glasses.

After a while it became just a question of keeping the bikes upright and applying power evenly so the rear wheels didn't slip. The snow was several inches deep—much deeper where it was drifting—and we weren't cutting through it. Whatever traction there was came from the compressed snow under the tires. Often the bikes would slide, and we wavered around regaining our balance. We tried to ride as straight as possible, because that way we had the least danger of falling.

We had to lean into the crosswind, too, which wasn't helping with the traction problem at all. When I stopped to take a picture, sheltering the camera from the driving snow with my body, I was shocked at the way Lolly and Bill looked, riding tentatively along very slowly, wavering, leaning way out into the wind. No wonder we almost dumped the bikes every time the gusts slackened suddenly.

The road would have made a good track for snowmobiles. Slowly, almost painfully, we picked our way along. The snow continued for a couple of hours, and then we rode through slush on the pavement as the snow began to melt. It was hard riding, and Bill and I both agreed with Lolly that we should call it a day when we reached the little town of Driggs. Here the same motel chain that had shunned us in West Yellowstone welcomed us, and gave us their finest room. Do people make all the difference? I think they do.

While Lolly soaked in the tub, getting rid of the chill remaining from the day's ride, Bill and I went to check road and weather conditions at the local sheriff's office. Each person we talked to tried hard to be helpful—and each gave us a different opinion. We finally gave it up and went to dinner at the local bowling alley. An excellent salad bar packed in ice was uniquely held in a large, cast-iron bath tub complete with four clawed, cast-iron feet and a gold faucet. The waitress was a bubbling girl of about nineteen, home from her first year at BYU for the summer. She wanted to hear all about our trip, and she was surprised to hear we had come through the storm that day. We were already looking back on it, hardly able to believe we had ridden in those conditions.

We returned to the motel to write our logs, and Lolly checked her electronic odometer. Only 29 miles. It was the shortest day yet, I thought. We normally rode that far between breakfast and our first snack. Yet it had taken all our energy to keep the bikes moving through the snow. Part of me was proud that we had been able to do it, but part of me kept calculating how far behind our schedule we were falling. Not only were we facing the extra distance of the detour, but the weather was cutting into our daily mileage more and more. We were counting on the flat plains country somewhere ahead to help us make up the difference.

The Bakery in Driggs the next morning affirmed our Pancake Postulate. We were up early, and it looked like a sunny day. During breakfast, we discussed an alternate route: we could cross Teton Pass, rumored to be a scourge of bike riders, or follow along the Snake River as it made a long, leisurely semicircle westward. One of the ranchers in the cafe told us there was eight inches of snow on Teton Pass. Before we left The Bakery, we bought cinnamon rolls and bear claws for snacks later. We may have been undecided on the route, but we were unanimous in the snack selection.

The two routes diverged at Victor, a small town we reached in mid-morning, so we couldn't delay the decision. An old pickup passed, then made a U-turn and stopped beside us.

"Saw you as I went by," the driver said, smiling. "I'm Gene Forsyth. I ride bike around here."

"Hi, Gene. Glad to meet you." I explained our dilemma about the two routes.

"The river route is almost level," he said, "but I'd take the pass if I were you. It is pretty steep for a ways, but it's much shorter."

"How about snow?" Bill asked.

"Should be gone by now," Gene said. "Good riding to you!" He pulled away.

"What do you think?" I looked at the others. "Personally, I think we should go over the pass."

Lolly and Bill agreed. We were filling our water bottles when Lolly remembered the post office.

"Our mail is at Canon City, Colorado," she said. "And we're not going through Canon City now."

The postmaster at Victor helped us fill out a forwarding request, re-routing our mail to Eads, Colorado. Then we rode out of town towards the mountains.

A stream rushed from its watershed high on the timbered slopes ahead and slowed to a comfortable pace on the valley's alluvial bed. Our road paralleled the stream as we approached the first upwards gradient.

"Oh, no, look at that!" Lolly said, pointing to a huge sign indicating ten-percent grades and snow ahead. Passing the sign, we began the climb.

"Whew!" I was out of breath. We were halfway up Teton Pass, and each of us had been tacking—switching back and forth across our lane to decrease the grade. Of course we could only do this when no traffic was nearby. We rested several times, jamming the bikes against a steel guard rail to keep them upright.

Halfway up, we passed two fellows hitchhiking beside the road, carrying skis and poles. They had skied down from the summit that morning, and now were hoping to catch a ride back up so they could make another descent. As we pedaled past, we joked with them about not having room for them on the bikes. A short time later, they waved to us from the back seat of a car heading up the hill.

Even though climbing the pass was eating time, I knew we were on a great shortcut that would save us both time and distance. A couple of hours later, we were on the summit at 8,400 feet, watching people ski in the sparkling, dry powder snow. Beyond them we could see the mountainside sloping down sharply towards Jackson, Wyoming.

The east side of Teton Pass offers the kind of descent that makes you glad you have good brakes. Swooping down steeply, glad for our Gore-tex suits, we concentrated on riding straight across the icy spots and missing the patches of sanding gravel that would upset the bikes. Easy on the brakes, now, I thought, letting up on the pressure momentarily, but don't let it run away. Squeeze down again with the hand levers as the bike quickly picks up speed. Easy does it.

I heard Lolly and Bill shout the moment I saw the boulder bounding towards me off the bank. It rolled ponderously to a stop in my lane just after I passed, much too close for comfort. A shower of smaller rocks followed, scattering across the highway. I looked back up the hill while Lolly and Bill stopped and rolled the larger ones out of the road. Then we completed the ride down, passing through some sharp, walnut-sized gravel on the pavement just before the road leveled out. Lolly's luck ended here; she hit some of the sharp rocks and had a flat from the resulting rim cut, her first since the ride began 1,400 miles back.

Nothing was quite so welcome as the tailwind on the east side of the mountain. Wilson and Jackson were soon far behind us, and we stopped in Hoback Junction just long enough to get a snack in a little combination country store and cafe.

"Can you make good milkshakes?" I asked the proprietor. He looked as if he had a sense of humor.

"Just the best ones you've ever tasted," he replied, rising to the challenge.

We bantered each other for a moment, and then he produced three huge shakes, so thick they wouldn't go through a straw. He was right. If these weren't the best we'd ever had, they were close. It must have been the homemade ice cream.

The Teton Range fell quickly behind, turned by our rapid dash south from an overpowering presence when we were at its base to just an occasional glimpse in the rearview mirror. The tailwind continued its help as we headed southeast up the Hoback River drainage. It was a pleasant road to ride, climbing up a couple of hundred feet above the river to cross a steep ridge, then sweeping back to river elevation in a series of banked curves. The afternoon warmed a little, and bicycling became more enjoyable than we had known it for many days. The snowy Gros Ventre Mountains formed an inspiring backdrop to the east. This was more like it, I thought; this was what we had imagined before we left on the trip.

Basalt cliffs and steep banks bordered the river along much of the way, while occasionally water-sculptured rock or tuff provided interesting shapes and colors. We saw several places where avalanches and mud slides had rocketed down the steep slopes and across the road. At one place, hundreds of trees still green and lush were piled in a twisted, tortured heap beside the river where a snowy behemoth had torn them from the hillside and deposited them a few weeks before.

When Bondurant, the only name on our maps for many miles in either direction, appeared far up the valley, it was getting late in the day. Hoback Cafe and Cabins, built of logs that seemed to blend right in with the sage flats and emerald meadows, was prominent in the collection of structures we could see as we rode in. We rented a log cabin and went into the cafe for dinner.

It was the kind of cafe that has a bird's nest between every rafter on the outside and inside makes you feel warm and welcome with clean floors, lots of varnished knotty pine, and paintings of the Old West hanging on the walls.

And Bill Smith was just the sort of man you would expect in a place like this. He was the public-relations half of the Smith family, while his wife tended more to the kitchen. Bill did some guiding of hunters in the fall and was prominent in the area. When the locals occupied stools to talk, Bill was there with them, absorbing and contributing to the gossip. Bill had quite a line and a way of handing it to you that made you like it. We also liked the meal his wife fixed for us.

After dinner, leaving our gear in the cabin, we gathered the energy to get back on the bikes and ride the half-mile length of Bondurant. There were a few scattered homes, a church, post office and fire hall, many of the same log construction that gave the place its flavor. By the time we got back to the cabin, the light was fading and a pink alpenglow halo sat atop the Gros Ventres. Across the road in a meadow, a huge silver badger worked back and forth looking for rodents, reflecting the fading light every time he turned.

It was cramped inside the log cabin, with barely enough space to move around after we got the bikes inside. The wooden bed frames had a deep "US" branded into the footboards. Possibly World War II, I thought, maybe older. The tin, Montgomery Ward shower stall drummed with a metallic sound when you ran the water, but at least it was hot. Lying back writing in the logs, we talked about how it felt to be in Wyoming, and back on a road that paralleled our original route. Our plan was to ride southeast until we reached Interstate 80, then ride east to intercept the route. That way, we would minimize the extra distance caused by our detour. We finished writing the logs, and soon I heard Bill breathing long and slow. Lolly was already asleep.

For me the day had been fun. We had crossed the pass, and continued on for a long day, making 66 miles. Even with the steep climb up the pass, it was an enjoyable ride. The scenery was magnificent, and a tailwind had helped us all afternoon. But to me the main thing was that we were headed in the right direction again; we had a chance to catch up with our schedule. I had come to think about the ride in terms of making the average mileage so Bill would be able to finish with us. I lay there for quite a while, thinking. In the open country along Interstate 80, we should have a stiff tailwind. With those conditions we could soon make up the mileage shortfall and pile up enough margin to allow shorter riding days, or even a day off. My last thought before falling asleep was of a day not pedaling.

The next morning, fueled by Bill Smith's pancakes, we pushed along at 18 miles an hour. None of us wanted to mention the fine tailwind, superstitiously afraid that naming it might scare it away. But we were certainly aware of it even though its push was not enough to do much but offset some wind resistance. Let it keep up, I thought, this is great!

Lolly, with her sharp eye for game, spotted three moose along the road, one a small bull standing in a beaver pond—until we came within eighty yards. With that odd, distance-devouring gait all moose display, he lumbered into the timber and disappeared. Lolly always spotted wild creatures before I did; I like to think this was because I was watching the road and our track more carefully but that was not always true. Lolly just has good eyes.

We were gaining elevation slowly as we rode towards Pinedale. It was noon before we approached town, and we could see some activity going on beside the highway. At first we couldn't make out what it was, but soon we recognized a huge, colorful big top being erected. Three-man gangs of men were driving steel stakes into the ground with sledge-hammers, striking alternately with a steady rhythm. The stakes would sink visibly with each staccato blow, in tune with the hammer-and-steel dance of the men. We stopped to watch and I dug out the camera. Then a commotion under the canvas drew our attention, as an elephant went calmly about raising the tent poles with quiet confidence. Clearly, this was not the first time it had put up the tent.

The sign advertising buffalo burgers at the Charbroil Restaurant was more than we could resist. Besides, the thought of eating buffalo meat in the middle of this wild-west town seemed appropriate. The burgers weren't juicy, but they had a good flavor, and to top off the experience, we came out of the restaurant to find what seemed to be an elephant race in progress.

The police had blocked off Main Street, a four-lane thoroughfare these days, and six or seven elephants were lumbering back and forth giving rides, and engaging in non-competitive shuffles. It seemed a little weird, but then again we had run into stranger things. We rode away from the blaring circus loudspeaker and stopped at a supermarket at the south end of town.

We needed peanut butter, bread, jelly and energy bars. This store had a good selection of the kind we liked, so we stocked up. Lolly also bought oranges and bananas, which I packed in the plastic bag strapped on top of my sleeping bag. I noticed people staring at us as we arranged our loads, and suddenly I realized they were staring at our laundry. Tied onto the rear of each bike were a pair of socks, underwear and riding shorts, arranged to flap in the wind to dry out. We had evolved the practice of doing laundry each night and drying the items on the bikes the next day. We were accustomed to this, but evidently the people of Pinedale weren't.

South of the town is high desert plateau, ideal habitat for antelope. We saw hundreds of the animals, singly, in pairs and small herds. Some were quite near the road, and others we could barely make out as white and beige specks in the distance. Lolly made a game out of shouting at them as we rode by. If they were within a quarter of a mile of us, they would invariably wheel and dash away at her shout. Then, likely as not, they would stop or come trotting back.

We could see the dust ahead for several miles before we reached the construction zone, and then we were riding on gravel, the bane of the light touring bike. We bumped along, feeling each unevenness in the surface. Round, loose gravel like marbles tried to skid our wheels sideways and dump us. Ahead, we could see no end to the construction zone. The pounding was hard on our seats, already sore from hours in the saddle that day, but it was harder on our hands. The shock from the rough surface was transmitted through the front fork and the handlebars directly to our hands. No amount of shifting grips could lessen the numbing, aching effect. Added to the discomfort in my hands was my worry about our tires. Even if we escaped pinching a tube and getting a flat as we rode over the hard, projecting rocks, we were certainly doing damage to the tires. Would a cluster of flats overtake us later as a result of tiny rim cuts from the gravel? We also had to contend with rocks thrown up by passing cars, sort of like charging a position defended by slingshots. You keep your mouth shut, certain that a fist-sized boulder will fly up and knock your teeth out. Finally the gravel ended.

By the time we reached Boulder, we began to sense a high-mileage day in the making. It was early afternoon, and the light tailwind was still with us. A road sign proclaimed the next town to be Farson, 49 miles distant.

The easiest way for me to make real mileage on a bicycle is to go into a daydreaming state that shuts out thoughts of remaining distance and aching bottoms and palms. This is the way, so far, I have managed to ride against headwinds and up hills. Instead of letting conscious thoughts of the discomforts and frustrations dominate, I just concentrate on pedaling and keeping the speed up to whatever level I can sustain. After a while, you get so you can judge the output your body can sustain over a long period, and you do it automatically. My mind is free to wander and think about other things, and yet I remain alert to picking the track and to any traffic nearby. It was this detached state that had let Bill and me discuss some of the fine points of computers while we were pedaling over Lolo Pass a week and a half ago, taking the mountain in stride without suffering too badly from the climb. In this way, each in his own thoughts, the three of us rode southeast.

We were pretty tired by three o'clock, so we stopped for a snack and rest at a spot where we could lean the bikes against a highway marker and lean back on the grassy bank, viewing the wild and rugged wall of the Wind River range, rising apparently almost vertically from the plains many miles distant. Later in the afternoon an elevated butte came into view some distance ahead, and on it, silhouetted against the sky, was some sort of man-made object we couldn't identify. Our pedaling brought it closer and closer, and finally we could see that it was a man, a covered wagon, and a horse.

"Sherpheeder," Bill said.

"What?"

"I mean," Bill said slowly, "sheepherder."

We found the incident revealing, even then. From then on, whenever we wanted to emphasize that fatigue might be affecting our thinking, we would look at each other and say, "Sherpheeder."

Sitzman's Motel in Farson looked awfully good when we rode in at 7:30 that evening. We bolted down baked chicken and salad at the Oregon Trail Cafe with the kind of hunger only riding 104 miles in a day can create. Our conversation was animated. This was more like it! A couple of days like this, and we would be back on schedule as if we had never detoured. I felt a lot better about the time we were making. Tomorrow, we would reach Interstate 80 and turn east.

*May 25–May 31*

# 9

# HEADWINDS

FARSON, WYOMING–EADS, COLORADO

We were pumping along Interstate 80, eastbound across Wyoming. Sagebrush and spring grasses extended over rolling hills, conspiring together to keep the horizon at great distance. There was absolutely nothing in any direction to stop the wind. We were moving at 6 miles an hour, and I was hurting. Physically and mentally. But the worst part was that I began to have doubts that we could finish the ride.

If you research wind patterns across our country, you will find that a fairly dependable flow moves from west to east. Meteorologists will tell you this is the prevailing wind pattern. It was this information that helped us decide to ride from Oregon to Virginia instead of the reverse. Yet it was becoming evident that something was wrong. Not only were the winds no help, a relentless headwind blowing right down our throats had become the focus of our lives.

We were between Rawlins and Laramie, and I had just pulled around Bill to take my two-minute stint in the lead position, feeling the unobstructed force of the wind like a flexible but impenetrable wall. The pedals seemed to push harder against my feet, and while I could ride against the wind, knowing that I would be up in front for even a brief time was disheartening. Unconsciously I selected one of the metal marker stakes along the shoulder that appeared to be a two-minute ride away. I concentrated on that particular post and pedaled toward it. It wasn't supposed to be like this, of course. The last few days, in spite of everything I could do to remain positive, feelings of resentment had been creeping into my mind. What we were experiencing was so vastly different from our expectations. Several days had passed since that last good-mileage ride to Farson. From then on, as we headed southward through country thick with sage and antelope to intersect Interstate 80 at Rock Springs, the wind seemed to be acting on diabolical orders to do its utmost to hinder us. As we rode along, we had to overcome its growing force.

I had been leading for perhaps thirty seconds now, and already my lungs were flipping coins with my leg muscles to see which was tiring most rapidly. One-fourth of my stint down, three-fourths yet to go, as one of the metal markers slid by on the right side.

The minute we had turned east on the wide, smooth freeway shoulder at Rock Springs, my heart sank. For days—weeks, it seemed—we had been telling ourselves that as soon as we headed eastward we would have some help from the wind. The roaring in my ears would have been proof enough of the wind's speed even if my burning lungs weren't gasping out an SOS.

Thank you, Eighteen-wheeler, you can go by again if you want to and create another blast of air that just for a minute goes the same way we're going. And thanks for waving, too. Thank goodness the shoulder is wide and we can get several feet away from the high-speed traffic. Wind doesn't seem to bother cars . . . another metal post goes by on the right. Is this post going slower than the last one? Why do my thoughts focus on such small things?

I don't even care what the scenery looks like along this stretch; the only important thing is the wind. Pedaling along, I think back to yesterday—or was it the day before?—when we stayed in Rawlins and the motel owner took us to a laundromat in her car. It was the first time in three weeks we had moved under other than our own power, and the three-block ride seemed strange and wonderful, almost as if we had never been in a car before. We were stopping late and getting to bed as soon as possible, only to get up early and on the road again to make as much mileage as we could against the wind. Even so we were falling steadily behind our goal. In Rawlins we had been almost too tired to notice the signs of a boom town diminished in a few years to half its former size. Wyoming isn't helping us . . . it's trying to kill us.

Thank you for waving, Car. Lots of people are waving to us along this stretch, almost as if they know what we're going through and want to help. That railroad engineer who sent blast after blast from his whistle rolling across the plateau while he waved at us—was he a cyclist too? Did he know that we faced the same specter every day and were trying to keep from getting discouraged?

Thank you, Metal Post, for moving by no matter how slowly. Isn't my two minutes about up, haven't I been up here in the lead long enough? Has the little clock taped to Bill's handlebars stopped? I don't know if I can keep up this pace much longer. Is this really worthwhile, this riding across the country? What if we don't make it all the way across by the time Bill has to get back? Where will he fly home from? How close will he be to making it all the way?

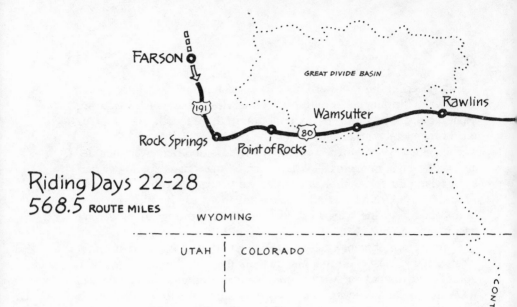

FARSON

GREAT DIVIDE BASIN

Rawlins

Wamsutter

191

80

Rock Springs

Point of Rocks

# Riding Days 22-28
## 568.5 ROUTE MILES

WYOMING

UTAH | COLORADO

CONTINENTA

How many times do we have to cross the Continental Divide, any-way? How come the air at 7,000 feet is so thin to breathe and so thick to ride against? You know, I am really getting tired of this, the hurt and the lung burn and the leaden ache of overworked leg muscles. Why don't we just stop? The prevailing winds aren't here, and they aren't going to be, at least not for us. This isn't enjoyable—the best thing that has happened for two days was that yellow school bus going the other way whose lady driver picked up her loudhailer and asked us, "Are you having any fun?" The waves and smiles she got back were counterfeit because we weren't having any fun with the winds.

How big were those pancakes at the Oregon Trail Cafe in Farson . . . big as the plate? Were they the reason we rode better until turning east on the freeway? Interstate 80 cafes along here leave a lot to be desired; maybe I'm just wearing down from lack of proper diet, maybe that's why it's taking so long for that next marker to get here. Maybe I'm wearing out, like that rear tire we changed on Lolly's bike yesterday—worn out, and now we're one spare short. And I know Lolly's game of counting the number of cars that wave to us is just something to do to keep our minds off of the riding effort. I know Lolly is hurting and she will have to stay behind Bill and me because she shouldn't have to face this wind.

Thank you, Eighteen-wheeler, and you, too—that helped, and maybe now I can make it to that marker. I know Bill's clock has stopped but if the trucks keep going by I can make it anyway. The wind is getting worse. It was 7,800 feet at Arlington and some of the names on the map here in Wyoming don't have towns. That rancher we met at our last rest stop didn't have to tell us that the wind is usually in the opposite direction. We can see the treetops bent towards the Atlantic, but their

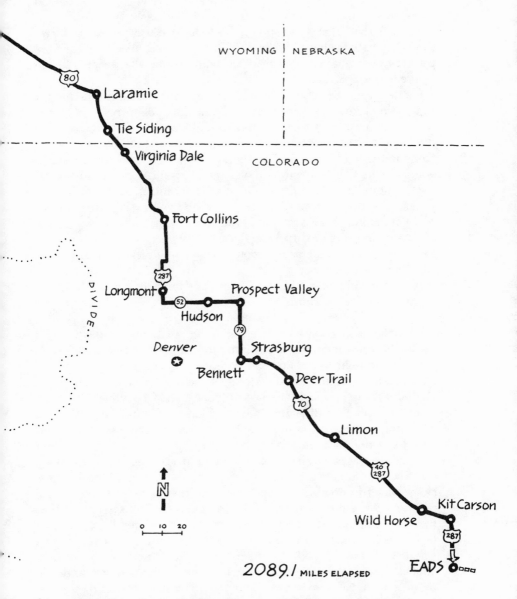

2089.1 MILES ELAPSED

thinner branches now point the other way, like a runner bent over and moving ahead with both arms streaming out behind him. Another rest stop is a good idea but I don't see any place out of the wind.

I'm sure of it now. I don't want to keep going any more because our ride is not worth this sort of torture. Bill isn't going to take the lead and even if he was, his clock has stopped and I'll have to stay up here who knows how long. Why couldn't this easting be as we had planned it, why are we battling so and still unable to make our average? Maybe we should go back to that crossing and buy that old Pontiac with the $200 price tag on it and just load the bikes in and see how far east it will run before it falls apart.

Laramie can't be too many miles farther, but what good is that if I can't even make it to my marker? At Laramie we will turn south, ninety degrees at least, and that's bound to make a difference in the wind direction. Maybe we should just keep fighting it and when we get to Laramie the worst we will have is a crosswind. I am willing to keep going or I am willing to stop if Lolly and Bill want to stop. I can almost see the number on that marker now. Is it my imagination or does the plateau slope down towards Laramie ahead? Well, whether it does or not, I am going to have to stop because my lungs and legs won't take any more and it's not surprising because I've been up in the lead a lot longer than two minutes and I don't know why I picked a marker that was so far away, anyway.

And then Bill pulled by, and I dropped into the blessed relief of drafting tight behind him.

We replaced our spare tire at a bike shop in Laramie, and shipped a package home containing used-up maps and a few other items. Then we spent an hour in the Rose Steak House, lunching on their special, and as far as possible let the strain of the last few days drain away. Highway 287 to Denver lay to the south of us, and for a while at least, we would ride in that direction. Our memories of those days crossing Wyoming in the wind would remain sharp even though our lungs and muscles were rapidly returning to normal.

The place was run by a Chinese family, and a happier, more animated clan you couldn't imagine. From the sparkling, black-eyed toddler mischievously grinning to the aged couple of generations back, here was a real live-wire group. If they had cares, you would never suspect it as they laughed, kidded and worked. The place itself literally shone, and they gave it human warmth and a magical, uplifting atmosphere that was just what we needed. It was good to learn that we weren't immune, after all, to our fellows. When we finally rode out of town around two in the afternoon, we were in better spirits than we had been for days. Even better, we had a tailwind.

Highway 287 was a narrow road, but on this section traffic was light. Because we could see trucks coming and get off the pavement before their bow waves hit us, we got by nicely. The last thing on our minds was meeting another cyclist, but the figure approaching us far in the distance was unmistakable. We could see legs pumping, and as the gap between us closed the rider rapidly grew larger. You could sense the anticipation on each side at finally talking to a bicyclist, and we crossed the road to wait on the shoulder.

"Hello," called Lolly.

The lone cyclist pulled to a stop and got off his bike.

"Hi," he said. "I'm Bill Atchley."

Introductions all around, talk edging quickly toward origins.

"I'm from Dallas, Texas," Bill said. "My brother is in Newberg, Oregon, and I'm headed there for a visit."

We told him we had started from the Oregon coast not far from Newberg.

"Have you had much wind?" I asked, trying to get an idea of what lay ahead.

"I'll say!" our new acquaintance said. "I've been making about 120 miles a day. Best tailwind you could imagine!"

We told him that if conditions remained the same, he could count on an even better tailwind ahead. He looked fit and rested, not at all as we knew we must appear to him. It was also painfully clear that we were not to get much respite from the wind.

With a wave, we left Bill Atchley to his route, and continued south towards the Colorado line. Later in the afternoon, clouds gathered like a thin gray glaze on the sky, and our tailwind turned sour. Huge thunderheads were building around us, cottony white tops belying the threat of their dark bulk, and we began to feel the need to look for shelter. Drummond, Idaho, was still fresh in our minds. Once more we could find no readily identifiable protection from the increasing winds, and the weather looked more and more foreboding. Ranches were few in this stretch, and ahead of us, without forests on their lower foothills, we could see the mountains rising.

It didn't seem strange at the time, being run to ground by a storm that—except for a thirty-knot wind—had not yet arrived, and the group of buildings we were approaching looked mighty good. Our map said Tie Siding and soon we could make out a confirming sign by the small post office, which was closed. The gas pumps were deserted and the main building vacant. That left only the mobile home next door. My request for a place to camp was granted, but only after a close scrutiny of helmets, dark glasses and the three tired riders inside the garb. Apparently satisfied that we were authentic, Billy Pickel waved us into his fenced back yard.

The wind was manageable in the lee of the building, and we soon had the tents up and water on the stove. While waiting for it to boil we watched Billy's daughter put a couple of excellent Australian sheepdogs through their paces. We learned that Billy was a teacher in Laramie, teaching law courses to the upper elementary-grade students. Pre-legal law, he called it.

"Don't get near the kennels," Billy warned. "That red-colored dog will bite if it gets a chance."

I had no curiosity at all about that reddish dog, and I knew Lolly had even less. We admiringly watched the other well-trained dogs perform and by that time steam was rising from the pot on our tiny, roaring stove. Giving the kennels a wide berth, we went to get supper.

"I wonder how many dogs he has?" Bill asked.

"I don't know," Lolly responded, "but I'm not going near that kennel to find out."

We all three climbed into one tent to make eating easier and more fun. The wind dropped as darkness approached, but the boiling clouds were still waiting to pounce. Up near the tops of a couple was just the faintest trace of a burnished copper refraction. Maybe tomorrow would be a good day.

"Hey," Lolly said, "there's something dead outside the tent."

Inspection turned up a long-dead cat about three feet in front of the tent door.

"Let's throw it over the fence," Lolly suggested, shuddering.

But when we thought about it, the dried-out, mummified carcass seemed better left undisturbed.

We stayed awake barely long enough to write up our logs. Sometime in the middle of the night, we were awakened by the frantic barking of every dog in the kennels. Increasingly audible above the cacophony were the wailing songs of a number of coyotes out in the desert. Not really wanting to hear, but having no choice, we listened to the contest. The coyotes came very close, as if they knew the dogs were confined. The dogs, on the other hand, seemed insulted that their territory should be invaded by their wild cousins. They argued about it for a long time, each side sometimes taking its turn and sometimes trying to drown the other out.

At last the coyotes must have tired of the game and wandered off, because things quieted down. It was a draw; neither side had won. At first I thought we were the losers, being awakened, but then appreciation for the contest we had experienced overcame the thought. By the time we got up the next morning, Billy Pickel had already left for work, leaving a note on our bikes. It was a long commute to Laramie. We had promised to send him a picture of our camp in his yard, grateful that his cold scrutiny of our first meeting had assured him that we were harm-less and in need. We left a note of thanks on his door.

Those who travel by auto do not discover the significance of culverts, deep ditches and other drainage structures with which builders of highways protect the roadbed and carry off water. Ride a bike very long out across the desert, though, and you find yourself looking very in-tently for a clump of trees. Lacking that, you soon willingly accept a clump of bushes, and lacking that, you soon discover culverts. When nature calls, a culvert allows privacy from one's fellows, including fel-lows in cars who approach at high speed. There is something very conspicuous about a white bicycle helmet sticking up out of the sage-brush; at such times you soon learn to take your helmet off and enjoy the natural camouflage of the unprotected head. On long, straight stretches of desert, with never-ending, flat topography, it is the culvert that comes to the rescue of the rider.

The Highway 287 entrance to Colorado is at the end of a long uphill grade and at that elevation a few scraggly pines struggle for survival among the rock outcroppings. We took pictures at this entrance into our fifth state, then pushed off on a long, basically downhill ride that lasted all day. The light tailwind helped us through tiny though historically significant spots like Virginia Dale, Ted's Place (where we had a lunch of pancakes) and Laporte before we got into big-city traffic near Fort Collins. The traffic increase made it easy to decide to skirt the Denver area on the east, and before nightfall we had Loveland, Campion, Berthoud, Longmont, Frederick and Dacono all put away in our used map pocket. It was another century day, 100 miles ridden, when we finally quit riding at Fort Lupton.

Despite next day's mailing deadline for the newspaper column, I was too tired to do more than write up the log that evening.

Early the next morning I produced and mailed the column. Neutral winds that day let us pedal southward through central eastern Colo-rado, beside grain fields dotted with huge oil-well pumps nodding like praying mantises to the soil. The agriculture of the area appeared sound, but the sight of a dozen or so wells scattered through the grain out to the horizon made us wonder which resource was the primary one. Grain, of course, makes better bread.

Sometime during the day, approaching a stop sign where there was not much chance of traffic, I stopped in the road. Lolly, who had been following behind, rammed into the back of my bike. The impact didn't quite knock her down, but her bike was on the pavement by the time I looked around. Lolly was furious.

"Please," she said, "sing out when you're slowing or stopping. I can't watch traffic behind and you in front, too."

For weeks to come, that was the last time I, or Bill, seriously erred in calling out before we slowed or stopped. "Slowing. Stopping!" became familiar calls.

Hudson, Prospect, Bennett, Strasburg, Byers, Deer Trail and Agate prepared themselves in an orderly way for entry into our logs for the day, the second century day in a row. To celebrate, we had dinner at the Riverdale Restaurant, in Limon. We didn't quite know what to expect when we saw the sign that proclaimed an all-you-can-eat buffet for only $5.95. Rick Lively, the owner of the place, showed us. He had moved to Limon with his young family from Dallas, Texas. He had opened the restaurant, a family business, two weeks before, and the place was packed. Rick's wife did a lot of the cooking, and Rick circulated among the diners making sure everyone was happy. We were. The enchiladas, tacos, chicken, salad bar and sopapillas for dessert went down with ease and in quantity. We were in heaven—add the great meal to an afternoon with no headwinds to speak of, and you have a great day.

Back in the motel, we figured we were 87 miles from Eads, Colorado, our mail stop. Bill's wife, Connie, had planned on flying to meet us for a few hours while we were near Denver, so Bill arranged with her on the phone to meet the next evening. Connie would fly to Denver, rent a car and chase us down at Eads.

The next day it became apparent that we wouldn't get to Eads before the post office closed because our headwind was back in robust health. Again Bill and I were taking two-minute turns in the lead, grinding along at no more than 7 miles an hour. We wanted to get our mail, but we knew the next day was Saturday and the post office would be closed.

"Call the police department," Lolly suggested. "I'll bet they'd pick up the mail for us."

Bill did that and, yes, the police chief would be happy to get the mail and hold it for us. By the time we reached Eads it was after closing time, but a few queries soon located the police chief's home, and he did have our mail. His wife had picked it up. I guess he wondered what kind of people had made this strange request, but after we met him and his wife, and talked over how the Canadian geese were doing that year, and how life in a small town was going, we didn't seem strange to one another anymore. Bill left to meet Connie at the police station.

We stayed in town until around ten o'clock the next morning, when Connie had to leave. We had to leave, too, because each of us was aware of the distance ahead. We had come just over 2,000 miles, and it was farther than that to Virginia Beach.

# 10

# *THE PLIERS*
# *OF KANSAS*

EADS, COLORADO–LARNED, KANSAS

"Wow! Look at that!" Lolly indicated the pancakes on the huge, oval plates. "They're hanging over the sides!"

The waitress had assured us that the pancakes were large. Not only were these cakes adequate in the quantity department, they were just the right combination of fluffiness, with crisp, brown, concentric rings and edges that were done just right: real works of art that made you want to plop a gob of butter down on them and get to it. It wasn't that we were particular about the size of pancakes; but since they had become our staple breakfast, one that we could depend upon to give us enough fuel to ride strongly until at least mid-morning, we had become pancake experts. If the pancakes were small—less than eight inches in diameter—we would order double stacks. These were the largest pancakes we had seen.

"How do we handle this?" Bill mused, half to himself, and then answered his own question by boring a hole in the middle, filling it with strawberry jam, and digging into those delicious hotcakes, eating from the inside out. Lolly and I followed suit, having amazingly little trouble finishing the pancakes as well as the two eggs and four strips of bacon that came with them. The waitresses had been really friendly, like so many of the people we had met in Kansas, but now they had strange looks on their faces and were staring at us. Evidently most customers didn't even come close to finishing the pancakes. But then, most of the customers at the Cactus Patch Cafe in Tribune, Kansas, weren't bike riders.

The prior day, which had started for us in Colorado, had been short on miles and long on hours. Our headwinds were back with us, and we

84

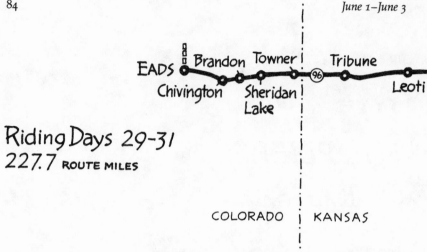

## Riding Days 29-31
## 227.7 ROUTE MILES

were trying to ignore them. There was little to see from that narrow strip of asphalt with the clay shoulders. Secondary Highway 96 leads eastward through sage flats that in June become the wide, seemingly endless grain fields that finally escorted us out of Colorado. To keep the mind alive, Lolly decided to count the vehicles that waved to us. Not those returning our waves, but those that waved first. The count represents a good percentage of all the vehicles along the route that particular Sunday—twenty-eight cars, four motorcycles and two railroad locomotives.

Kansas people gave us a good feeling, difficult to describe; they seem close to the earth itself, contented with where and what they find themselves to be. We didn't feel out of place or that the Kansas people were as reserved as some. I'm sure so many bicycle riders had been along this route in the past that we were no novelty; maybe that's why we felt accepted.

Chivington, Brandon, Sheridan Lake and Towner are tiny places on the map, but important commercial and social centers to the people who live there, and we had expected to find at least one cafe open for lunch. It had been raining intermittently, a cold rain that made hot food sound good, but all the "Closed" signs proclaimed that food simply wasn't served on Sunday afternoon. Luckily, Connie had left a good supply of chocolate-chip cookies with us. We munched these in the shelter of the local fire hall, keeping one eye warily on the darkening clouds and listening to the wind whistle by.

At the state line, Kansas welcomed us with a deluge. We had to put on full rain gear to have any chance at all of staying dry, but even that protection didn't do the job. Water sprayed up behind our front tires in

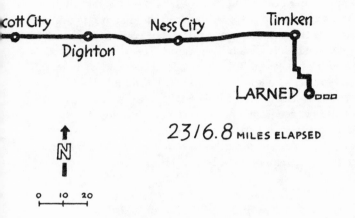

vicious streams intent upon soaking our feet; water cascaded off our helmets into the necks of our jackets. The Kansas precipitation continued with no let-up as we rode on through the afternoon. The mind starts wandering at such times, a protective mechanism to entrance you into false bodily comfort. I had time to think about Connie's report that one of the TV channels at home had just done an update on us and the ride. I vowed to take a roll of film and send it to them along with a more detailed story. The reports that the weekly column was a big success were gratifying.

Darkness and Tribune, Kansas, arrived at nearly the same time. The rain hadn't let up for a minute. We checked into a motel only to find water inside the plastic bag liners of our panniers and most of our gear wet. Luckily, our sleeping bag protection had not chafed through during the 2,100 miles since the Oregon coast, and the sleeping bags were okay. We dried the hard items with towels, spread all the rest of our stuff around the room, turned up the heat all the way and went out to dinner. After all, it was a celebration of sorts. Rain or no, sometime during the day we had passed the ride's halfway mark.

That night, we were shaken awake by the trembling of the ground and a roar that brought us, wide-eyed and hearts pounding, out of a sound sleep to discover that our beds were only yards from the railroad tracks.

Next morning, after those perfect pancakes at the Cactus Patch Cafe, we bought the heaviest plastic bags in the local supermarket. Taking them back to our room, we repacked our now-dry gear; this took some time, and meant we got away late.

A tiny, familiar-looking dot on the other side of the road rapidly took the form of a cyclist heading our way. A rider in the distance is unmistakable. You can't see the pedal motion at first, but you can see a short, wide body with legs that don't reach the ground. The intervening space closed quickly and we crossed to the other side of the road to intercept the rider. He was young, strongly built, and had a friendly but serious smile that crossed a freckled face topped with reddish hair that his helmet couldn't quite conceal. His name was Kevin Braun.

"I was wondering when I'd meet you," Kevin said, after we had introduced ourselves. "For days now, I've been telling myself that somewhere other riders are going along the route in the other direction. And here you are."

"Where did you start?" Bill asked.

"Yorktown, Virginia. I'm heading for the Oregon coast."

Well, we knew where that was, although it seemed an eternity since we had left on the ride.

"Have you had much wind?" Lolly asked.

"No, just a nice tailwind," Kevin said.

"Well, you should continue to have a tailwind, because we've had nothing but headwinds."

We learned that Kevin was from Wisconsin, where he worked in a cheese factory. At twenty-four, he was eating up the miles without difficulty, doing about 70 miles a day, roughly the same as our overall average. But somehow it looked a lot easier for him. It was obvious that meeting us was an emotional experience for him because of weeks of contemplation about when he would encounter riders going the other way, and who those riders would be. Travelling alone, he had seen things and had experiences that he wanted to share with someone. Meeting us, even though briefly, allowed an enthusiastic release, which we felt also. We talked for some time, learning about his job, and how he had decided to take time off from work in order to make his first big ride happen. We exchanged addresses, and with a wave we parted. Kevin pedaled away westward with his tailwind. We went east.

The rain that had been falling gently off and on during the day became warmer than any precipitation we had encountered so far. Whenever a light shower seemed sure to pass, we didn't put on our rain gear at all and instead just got wet. We dried out quickly enough as soon as the sprinkles stopped.

Just east of Leoti, the horizon-to-horizon grain fields began grudgingly to yield their choking hold on the landscape to scattered trees and twisting, shallow watercourses, relieving the monotony of the open plains. We began to notice a hint of odor, and within a few miles were aware of a definite aura that became permeating as the afternoon progressed. The realization grew that not only is wheat grown here, but at least some of that grain is fed to cattle. Lots of cattle. Soon numerous stock trucks were passing us, streaming vile liquid onto the wet roadway in clouds of evil-smelling spray. We tried to keep from breathing as long as possible after a truck went by. When we were finally forced to suck in a lungful of air, the thought of the bacteria floating around in it made us shudder. We all noticed a touch of diarrhea on this section of the trip—thanks, probably, to the spray thrown up from the cattle trucks. A few feed lots stood close to the road, but most are back on side roads, out of sight. Never were they far out of mind.

The wind died down for an hour in the middle of the afternoon. As we kept on pedaling, our speed increased to 15 miles an hour. What a thrill to sail along, covering lots of ground, with the same effort it took to do 8 miles an hour against the wind. After all, these were the plains of Kansas, where we were supposed to be zipping along with the prevailing wind at our backs. We talked about that for a time, and then the wind resumed and we didn't talk much at all for quite a while. I don't know about Bill and Lolly, but I was resentful. Not to the degree of giving up, as I had been tempted to do during the terrible Wyoming crossing, but resentful at having to battle so hard just to move along level ground when it didn't have to be that way.

For a month now we had been telling each other that the riding would be easy when we got to Kansas. Where *was* our tailwind? It sure wasn't buoying us along. We had reached the point where, upon getting up in the morning, the first thing one of us would do was to look at a tree, or bush or clump of grass, to see which direction the wind was blowing and how hard. The few weather maps we had seen en route showed stationary low-pressure areas in the western plains states, and it was this phenomenon that had dashed our hopes of crossing the country with the wind at our backs. But understanding the cause of the headwinds didn't make the riding any easier. So we just kept pedaling along, against the wind, across country where windbreaks are rare and the gusts can take a bead on you from a mile away.

When we met him east of Ness City, Jim Hoover was riding an expensive bike, equipped with expensive accessories and equipment. We had seen him coming for half a mile, and we stopped to talk. From Harrisburg, Pennsylvania, Jim at fifty-one had retired as an inspector in public assistance, and decided to take a long-distance bicycle tour while he was still able. Somewhere along the way he'd picked up a bad cold or virus infection, and he was really dragging, fresh out of enthusiasm of any kind.

"I call my wife every so often and let her know how I am," Jim said.

We learned he had ridden for a couple of days with Kevin Braun.

"That Kevin was too much for me. When I slowed down, he finally just went on ahead. I haven't seen him since."

We gave Kevin's address to Jim, since they had no easy way of reaching each other.

We realized how lucky we were. Travelling together and getting along well, we avoided the loneliness of the solitary riders we met. They had seen lots and overcome difficult things, but none of it could be shared with anyone, because no one else had experienced it.

"How have conditions been for you?" Lolly asked. I knew that she was thinking of headwinds.

"Well, the worst things I've had were the steep hills in the Ozarks," Jim said. "I couldn't ride up some of them."

We looked at one another. This was the first we had heard of steep grades, although I did recall reading an account where the rider had trouble with Ozark hills.

"Where are you headed?" I asked.

"Seattle," Jim said. "I hope I make it."

"Oh, you'll make it fine," Lolly said. "You should have good tailwinds from now on."

Lolly was trying to cheer him up, and judging from the half-smile on his face, the first since we'd met, it was working.

We had barely waved good-bye to Jim and watched him ride away when we passed a plaque marking the homestead of the great agricultural chemist George Washington Carver, a 160-acre tract on which Carver built a cabin when he was twenty-two years old. Still later, we came upon a row of fence posts made of stone. At first, I couldn't figure out what the post material was, and thought it might be wood or concrete. When we got closer it was easy to identify it as yellowish, lichen-covered stone. Six to eight inches square, the posts were probably around five or six feet long. Orderly rows of holes adorned opposite sides of the posts, where each had been painstakingly split off from slabs of some sort of sedimentary rock. Strands of wire encircling each post held barbed wire in position. It was evident that many of the posts had been in place for a long time, and had settled until sometimes little more than three feet of post projected above the ground. It occurred to me that you could probably tell the age of a fence by how far its posts had settled. We pondered the amount of labor that must have been required to make a post, but apparently there was little choice: few trees grew in the region. It seemed right to us that we didn't see any recently made posts. All appeared ancient hosts of varicolored lichen colonies—solid, weathered curiosities of the past whose years of service were attested by rusty strands of wire.

* * *

"Those two guys must be electricians," I said, indicating two men who had just arisen from a booth at the cafe where we were having the catfish lunch special. "See the pliers in those leather sheaths?"

Lolly and Bill glanced at the two, and then around the cafe. We noticed several other men in the place wearing pliers at their belts, but they didn't look like electricians at all. In fact, we watched the first two go out and climb into four-wheel-drive pickups. Ranchers, obviously. We didn't think much more about it until that evening, when pliers-toting men dominated the crowd in another little restaurant.

"What is this?" Bill wondered aloud.

One hefty, jovial fellow, resplendent in shiny western boots, embroidered shirt and expensive white Stetson, bore at his belt in a carefully oiled leather sheath a long-handled pair of pliers, chrome-plated. The man next to him, in blue jeans and a denim jacket, wore his pliers in a black leather sheath. In the course of half an hour, we saw blue steel pliers, lineman's pliers, shiny-plated pliers, and pliers with handles long and short. Belt sheaths came in different styles, too: some ornately tooled, some regular tan leather and some both tooled and dyed in designs.

We were in Scott City, and this was certainly the home-town crowd. Everybody seemed to know everybody else in the place. Because of our riding garb we stood out like sore thumbs, and it was a toss-up who stared most at whom. With all those pliers around us and everyone acting perfectly natural about them, we did our share of staring and speculating. These people were friendly, but none of them seemed ready to speak to us.

Finally, Bill asked one fellow about the significance of the pliers. It's a tradition, he told us. Probably a carryover from past times when fencing chores were forever cropping up and a man had to have a pair of pliers with him or he wasn't able to do his job. Today, the pliers are mostly a symbol of that heritage. From the apparently rigid adherence to the "can't be caught dead without your pliers" syndrome, all you would need to be accepted into rural Kansas society would be a fancy pair of pliers, a fancier leather sheath to carry them at your belt and, probably, to have been born in Dighton.

Log entry: "In spite of the headwinds, we have rolled our six tires across 96 miles of Kansas pavement today, and the eleven hours required to do that has installed an aching numbness in that part of us that contacts the bicycle seat. We used our head- and taillights for half an hour before we rode into Larned.

"Other than the wind situation, we are enjoying the ride. The countryside is less monotonous here and, finally, we are warm. No longer is the winter clothing we used in the Rockies needed; we can ship some items home. But the most gratifying thing is the Kansas people. We have had numerous offers of help, food and lodging. The local people have a certain sincerity of deed and action that we like. We even enjoy the status-symbol pliers and agree that Kansas is a friendly place."

Bill, Don, and Lolly ready to leave the beach at Neskowin, Oregon, on a 4,000-mile ride across America.

This camp, up a sheltered draw, offered protection from the wind in the Ochoco Mountains of Oregon.

Bill and Lolly climbing Mitchell Hill in eastern Oregon.

Greeted by a snowstorm when entering Montana at the summit of Lolo Pass.

Bill and Lolly have an afternoon snack of Andy's apple fritters near Jackson, Montana.

Deep snowbanks line the highway at Chief Joseph Pass, Montana, along the Continental Divide.

Riding at the tail end of a blizzard near Drummond, Idaho, in some of the most difficult conditions encountered on the trip.

The log cabin in Bondurant, Wyoming, came with lots of atmosphere.

Riding through the Bitteroot Valley, near Hamilton, Montana.

Weaving carefully through a cattle drive near Ennis, Montana.

Playing tag with storms over a pass near
Virginia City, Montana.

Laboring up Teton Pass, a 10% grade near
Jackson, Wyoming.

Patching a flat during a sunny spell near Mitchell,
Oregon.

The Clubb, Missouri, post office. In these parts some very small places show up on the map.

A heavy rainstorm was the welcome to Kansas, the Sunflower State.

Ferry crossing of the Ohio River into Kentucky.

Honesty and realism in road signs.

When coal trucks took the entire lane, it was time
to take to the dirt.

Bill, Don, and Lolly at the surf in Virginia Beach, at the end of their
4,150-mile ride across America.

*June 4–June 9*

# 11 🚴

# *IT'S A LONG WAY*
# *TO THE MISSISSIPPI*

LARNED, KANSAS–HARTVILLE, MISSOURI

The advice the owner of the bike shop in Larned gave us more than made up for the fact that he didn't stock tires in our size.

"The road is torn up through the Quivera Wildlife Refuge," he told us. "You'd be better off to detour south, through Hudson, and get back onto the route east of Hutchinson."

He helpfully marked our maps for us. We crossed the Arkansas River, and just seeing "Arkansas" on the road sign made us feel we had come a long, long way. The opposing wind slackened, and soon we were making 12 miles an hour along Highways 19 and 281. Then, as advised, we turned south to Hudson.

There are a lot of retired people among the 180-plus population of Hudson, where a towering flour mill proclaims "HUDSON CREAM FLOUR" on a huge sign high on the structure. Several local people were having lunch at the cafe when we entered. Even the usual reserve was lacking, and in a few minutes we found ourselves relating details of our trip to an interested audience. For some reason, the folks in Hudson didn't act as if we were from another planet.

In fact, we had trouble finishing our meal before the food became cold. We got more advice on the best route to Hutchinson, with some local navigational fine points that were really helpful. As we left town, people in their yards or on their porches waved to us. Maybe it was the large shade trees, the neat yards filled with flowers and closely cropped lawns, but I think it was the friendly people that made the little town of Hudson stand out.

Harley's Bike Shop in Hutchinson had an inventory. Our mouths dropped open when we walked through the door, for there in front of us was every sort of bicycle paraphernalia you could imagine. Our map guide had listed Harley's, but we had no idea we would find so many goodies in the shop. Lolly selected a special seat cover with space-age padding in hopes it would soften the effect of the bike seats. We also purchased a tire, to replace the spare we were short. And we talked with Harley.

"Being in the middle of the country, riders heading each way stop here," he said. "They all descend upon us in waves during the touring season, and then business drops back to normal for the remainder of the year."

It was easy to see he had lots of experience in helping touring riders.

"Would you like to stay at the hostel?" Harley asked. "It's just a few blocks down the street."

"Sure," Lolly said.

We learned that Harley, working through the Lutheran Church in Hutchinson, had been instrumental in establishing a hostel at the old parish house. Needless to say, many guests at the hostel were bicyclists who either learned of the hostel through listings in cycling guides, or were sent there directly by Harley. As we talked with him, the shop salesperson fell away to reveal enthusiasms and concern for our well-being. Harley was clearly an unusual person. The sincerity of his church work with young people and cyclists in particular was evidence enough even if you didn't happen to notice the mist in his eyes as he

## Riding Days 32-37
### 466.3 ROUTE MILES

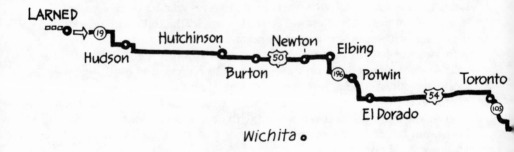

talked. He must have known we would appreciate a spot to stay, and Lolly's quick acceptance proved it.

The big, white two-story house that was the hostel looked homey and comfortable when we rode up. A church committee meeting was going on near the stairway, but the members, apparently accustomed to riders, motioned us up the stairs. The rooms were large and plain, but most important to us was that we could take showers and sleep on good beds. We sat on the iron deck of the second-story fire escape that evening, drinking in the cool breeze and writing in our logs.

"I rode from Denver to Hutchinson, Kansas, on a dare at my fortieth birthday," the man was saying to Lolly at the post office the next morning. I had been buying film while Lolly mailed home a package containing our long johns. Several people were standing around outside the post office, talking with Lolly and looking at her bike.

"I thought I would die," the man continued, "but like I said, I was forty, and tough. I'd hate to think about riding the distance you're going."

We learned that he had a business in Hutchinson, had been a forward air controller in Vietnam, and did a little bike riding once in a while. He was a private pilot now, too, and of course that struck a chord in Bill, who does quite a lot of flying. We had trouble getting away.

Highway 50 took us through Burrton and Newton, and a nightmare ride on Highway 196, where shoulders on the road were bad or nonexistent, brought us to El Dorado.

"ALL YOU CAN EAT—$5.79" said the sign at the Sirloin Stockade. The salad bar and entrees included everything you could think of. There were several kinds of potato and macaroni salads, lots of fruits, and every vegetable that is eaten raw or pickled, as well as a number that aren't. Beef, poultry and fish, prepared not one but several different ways, were stacked on steam tables. The cooked vegetable dishes of

2783.1 MILES ELAPSED

every sort made choosing difficult. But we tried. Even with a small helping of everything, we couldn't make it once around.

We were aiming for the carbos and proteins, but finally wound up at the dessert counter, which had pies, cakes, gelatins and puddings. All during our meal the waitress had been topping off our huge, quart-size glasses with a non-caffeine soft drink. Finally, we were having trouble polishing off the last of the chocolate pudding that remained on our plates. A man I took to be the manager wandered over.

"How can you make any money at that price?" I asked him.

He looked at us for a minute, and I could see the amusement in his eyes.

"We make money on some people, and lose a little on others," he said. "Not everyone who comes in is a bike rider."

I expected him to add, "Thank goodness," but he just smiled. "Don't forget the free soft ice cream cone when you leave," he chuckled. "The machine is over there. Just help yourselves."

Before we left the Sirloin Stockade, a young waiter who looked as if he might be working his way through school came over, and asked what we now called our W & W questions: *where* are you coming from and *where* are you going? I think the answers helped him correlate our thin waist-lines with the meal he had seen us eat.

It was difficult writing the column that evening in the motel. In spite of the amount of food we had been used to consuming, the gorged feeling from that dinner stayed with us for hours.

Next morning, while we were stopped at a rest area near Toronto, a familiar van approached us on Highway 39. We recognized the squarish red top, customized by Leslie and Gladys Downen. We had first met the Downens near Limon, Colorado, where we had each stopped at the same rest area. The Downens were on vacation, and during the last few hundred miles we had met on the road a couple of times. By now we felt we knew them.

Leslie was a mechanic, his skill the undoubted reason their older van sailed along so well. Gladys worked in a health food store near their home in Newton, Kansas. They were obviously enjoying their trip, because they took lots of side roads and made sure they didn't miss anything as they traveled. Excited descriptions of where they'd been and the things they'd seen poured out, the words rapid-fire and running together in their enthusiasm.

We shared some of the high points of our trip with them as they broke out cold soft-drinks from their ice chest. Strange, but we felt the acquaintance was stronger than just passing several times on the road would account for. Maybe we were hungry for someone to talk to, or maybe the Downens were especially nice people, or else a little of both. As we prepared to leave, we took pictures and exchanged addresses so we could stay in contact.

Little by little the countryside had been changing. We probably wouldn't have thought much of it except we suddenly found ourselves riding up a very steep hill. The flat plains were gone now, and more and more forest appeared. The temperatures had been climbing over a period of several days, and we found that our perspiration no longer evaporated. We were streaming wet every time we had to exert ourselves to get up a hill. From the descriptions we'd heard, clearly we were entering the Ozarks.

The first few steep spots were notable because they nearly brought our bikes to a complete halt. We began to estimate the percent of grade each time we encountered a particularly nasty hill. Even in the lowest gear, pedaling took so much pressure that it made your knees hurt. The temptation was great just to step off the bike and push it, but we had vowed that we would ride every foot of the way. So we kept going, hoping we were through the steepest part but always hearing from people we talked with about steeper hills ahead.

When we reached Chanute, Kansas, that evening, we had another century day behind us. And we had begun to see some new things. Box turtles suddenly seemed always to be trying to cross the road, and many met eternity on the blacktop. Lolly picked up dozens of the tortoises and took them across, trying to pay attention so as to take them the way they wanted to go. Hundreds were already smashed by cars. When we stopped for a snack at a small country store, there on the counter was a picture of a sixty-pound catfish, caught that morning in the nearby Verdigris River. For the first time on the trip, we began hearing the calls of bobwhite quail, and that morning, in a woodlot between bottomland corn and bean fields, we had seen our first cardinal. Its vermilion flash was so bright and in such contrast to the lush foliage as to be discordant. The creeks and rivers now ran muddy brown, so different from the clear mountain streams we had been taking for granted.

Chanute, Girard, Capaldo and Pittsburg are places that stick in a cyclist's memory because of the steep hills that separate them. Some of those grades make the streets of San Francisco pale by comparison, and we wondered how the roads could be driven in the winter if they were snow-covered. We remember Chanute particularly, however, because Chanute is where we broke with tradition—and had waffles for breakfast instead of pancakes. Unfortunately, they didn't do the job and we were unbearably hungry by nine in the morning.

* * *

June 8 was a Sunday that saw us thirty-five days on the road and 2,700 miles away from home. Chance circumstances made the day memorable for other reasons. We crossed the Missouri line in mid-morning, paying little attention to a station wagon parked at a wide spot with one bicycle beside it and some people standing around. Fifteen miles later, while we were stopped for snacks, a puffing young man came riding up from the same direction we had come.

"Hi," he said, pulling up to stop where our bikes were parked. Sweat dripped off the end of his nose. He looked just a little out of shape, as if he had not quite reached his weight-reduction goal, but he was as friendly as could be. He was also panting hard.

"I'm Walt James," he said. "I've been trying to catch you."

We introduced ourselves, glad to have a cyclist to talk with.

"You went by while I was unloading my bike at the state line."

We learned that Walt, at thirty-five, was a mailman in Riley, Kansas, was married, and had a son and daughter. We had passed the family's tearful farewell to Walt at the state line.

"I've been trying to get in shape," Walt admitted. "Been doing some riding as preparation. Now I'm headed for Washington, D.C., and I've got two weeks to make the trip."

That sounded familiar to us, having a time limit. Walt seemed like a nice person, and we could sense that he felt a little tentative starting out on his trip by himself.

"You're welcome to ride with us if you like," I said.

"Thanks."

Walt told us he had purchased a new bike for his trip to the nation's capital. As we packed up the snacks and started down the road, we noticed that he was having a little trouble keeping up with us. The level sections were fine, but on the hills he would drop behind, panting hard. Then, on the downhill spots, he would catch up or go roaring by. At one time he was more than a mile behind, but the sight of Lolly riding her fully loaded bike up the hills must have bothered him, because he made a real effort to catch up, and stayed pretty close to us after that.

We had a chance to visit more over lunch in Cooky's Cafe in Golden City, a famous local spot where you go when you want to eat more food and pie than you should. Walt didn't have any trouble eating lots of food. We learned that he was a Vietnam veteran, and had decided to make the ride from the Kansas-Missouri line to the Vietnam Memorial in Washington, D.C., as a tribute to some who hadn't been as lucky as he had. Besides, the ride would be a great adventure for him. It was clear, though, that his strong feelings about his war experiences motivated his ride. He needed to make this pilgrimage to the memorial.

Through the afternoon, every time we approached long, steep hills and tried to stifle our inward groans, the rest of us found ourselves smiling slightly at Walt's favorite expression: "Omigosh!"

Bill is the local policeman in Ash Grove, and he saw us coming.

"I'll bet you'd like to camp in the park," Bill said. "It's down the street there. The restrooms are behind the pool, and there's water by the pavilion. If it's going to rain, I'll come by and open the VFW hall."

Obviously many bicyclists had come through Ash Grove, but still the smooth green lawn looked inviting for tents. We watched Walt with interest as he carefully set up his tent and got out his gear. He had done a good job of selecting items to take on his ride, and only fumbled with the tent for a minute or two. He would become a seasoned tourer in no time. We all turned in then, and while it didn't rain, so we didn't have to move into the VFW hall, Bill did check on his guests at least once during the night.

We rode as a group of four the next morning, enjoying Walt's company. We learned that he had been in law enforcement before becoming a mail carrier, but that profession hadn't suited him. He did like working for the postal service, and found his walking delivery route enjoyable—except for the dogs. Our own encounters with dogs had been few so far, but the incidents were increasing here in Missouri. As if on cue, a wiry-haired brown dog charged at us as we went by, apparently sensing Walt's occupation even though he was on a bicycle. Bill and I immediately went into our protective formation, dropping back to form a screen so Lolly could sprint on out of the way. We noticed that Walt followed her. As usual, the dog wasn't interested in us, it wanted to get at those two frightened ones up front who were getting away. A sharp rebuke and the wave of a tire pump discouraged the animal. The dogs were getting tougher, and more numerous.

The road through the small towns of Walnut Grove, Fair Grove and Marshfield was a roller coaster. We heard Walt's "Omigosh" many times after coasting down into the hollows, as we faced laboring up the other side in our lowest gear. Even in the gear Bill called his "stump puller," many of the hills were real strainers. Walt was doing better, conditioning himself along the way.

Lazy Louie's Bike Camp is well known to thousands of bicyclists. We met Louie that afternoon. Now in his eighties and beset with poor health, Louie was still cheerful and enthusiastic as he showed us around the modest buildings that have offered shelter to so many. Hundreds of postcards, mementos from past visitors, covered sections of the walls. Most of the other space was occupied by trinkets and gift items that Louis did his best to sell to us. If nothing else, Louie was a salesman. We declined his invitation to camp there because it was still early afternoon, and Walt had already gone on ahead.

The motel in Hartville had gone out of business, and after catching up with Walt, we inquired at the only other place to stay, a bed-and-breakfast inn. The quoted rates did not appeal to us—but after 77 miles of yo-yo, up-and-down riding, we could not go any farther.

"You can camp down by the swamp," the deputy at the police station told us. "Just go over the bridge leading out of town. It's down on your left."

We nodded our thanks and were about to leave.

"Be careful if you go in the water, though," he added. "There's lots of weeds and brush below the surface. It's dangerous."

We turned to leave.

"Hasn't anybody drowned there since that fellow last week," the deputy offered. "We found him right away."

"Thanks," Bill said.

A recently mown grassy area stretched to the water, so we had a sporting chance to see anything that crawled about the same time it saw us. We pitched our tent camp again, the damp heat making us wish for some way to get more ventilation through the sturdy tents. We talked with Walt for a while before the bugs drove us under cover. We knew his intended route branched off from ours somewhere ahead, but we hadn't pinned down the exact spot. It was fun riding together, because Walt's perspective was different from ours, and ours was understandably predictable to each of us after thirty-six days of riding together and seeing the same things in the same way.

The humidity in camp kept us from sleeping well, and we were up early, only to find Walt already had his camp practically packed.

"Have some orange juice?" I offered.

"No, thanks," Walt said. "I'm going to get an early start and see if I can make it to Eminence today."

"Okay."

It was evident that Walt wanted to get on the road. We had seen his confidence increase immensely during the past two days. He had also increased his riding endurance. Eminence was nearly 90 miles away by that same narrow road that one minute rewarded with thrilling, high-speed coasts and the next punished with impossible, ligament-tearing climbs. We sensed that Walt wanted to face his challenge by himself, just as we had been doing. And something deeper, something we might never know, seemed to be driving him on his personal pilgrimage to the Vietnam Memorial. Before we finished breakfast, Walt had gone.

*June 10–June 15*

# 12

# AGAINST
# THE HILLS

HARTVILLE, MISSOURI–LEITCHFIELD, KENTUCKY

The van had "Herbalife" painted all over it and we couldn't very well miss seeing it because we were grinding up one of those knee-busting Ozark hills at no more than 4 miles an hour, pulling hard with our hands and arms on the handlebars to create enough pressure to move.

"I'll meet you at the top!" the driver shouted, slowing as he went by going downhill.

We looked at one another with what were the best quizzical looks we could muster while pedaling so hard.

"Wonder what that's all about?" Bill asked.

"Maybe he wants to talk," Lolly said.

"There's three of us, anyway," I said. "Let's pull over at that wide spot on the crest and wait for him."

In less than a minute, the van came back up the hill, and pulled into the wide spot on the shoulder. The man who bounced out was exuberant, and smiling widely as he came over.

"I'm Art Bowlby," he said, shaking hands enthusiastically as we introduced ourselves. "Where are you from?"

We told him, adding that we were heading for Virginia Beach.

"I've ridden across the country twice," Art volunteered. "You're all carrying too much weight on your bikes. Twenty-one pounds is a good maximum."

I knew that Lolly was still packing twice that on her bike, and I had nearly three times that much. To be as light as twenty-one pounds was a noble goal.

"Let me get you some ice for your water bottles!" Art said suddenly.

He opened a plastic cooler chest, and fished out some ice cubes, which he dumped into the water bottles we eagerly held out to him.

Riding Days 38-43
468.1 ROUTE MILES

Only the blind and deaf could miss Art's enthusiasm when he talked: it showed in his body movements and on his face. He appeared to be in his mid-fifties, just a little on the plump side, with graying hair and just a trace of accent that I couldn't quite pin down.

"I'm from Nova Scotia," Art offered. "Been a lot of places and done a lot of things."

He finished with the ice cubes, and rustled around in the cooler some more.

"Here, have some nectarines," he said.

While we ate the cold, juicy fruit, Art filled us in on some of his experiences. He had been active in the American Youth Hostel organization at one time. He was also a blue-water sailor, he told us, and we might have been just a bit skeptical except that the things he said rang true. It was obvious that he had lived an adventurous life.

The badge Art was wearing read: "I'VE LOST 43#—ASK ME," but we didn't. For one thing, we were trim to the point where losing weight held no appeal—and for another, Art had a ways to go himself.

But his enthusiasm was catching, and we were soon talking about all sorts of adventures. I glanced over at his van occasionally, and noticed quite an assortment of gear inside. Probably the Herbalife distributorship was his main endeavor now, but we didn't ask about that. It was enough to enjoy exposure to the man himself, and by the time we felt we should be getting along, our spirits had received a real boost. You couldn't spend much time with Art Bowlby without some of that exuberance rubbing off on you.

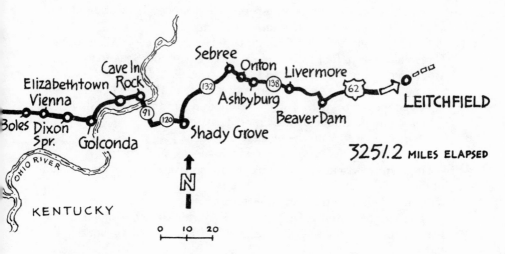

"You'll like the campground on Clearwater Lake," Art said. "It isn't far from here."

We thanked him for his kindness, and watched as he turned the van around in the same "full speed ahead" way that he talked, and within seconds the vehicle bounced onto the roadway and disappeared over the crest of the hill. Art Bowlby had come into our lives abruptly and disappeared the same way, but the encounter left us better off—a wave of enthusiasm that you couldn't help but absorb. We were smiling again, the hurt in our knees forgotten.

We had been paralleling the Gasconade River that morning, the even grade of the small valley a welcome change from the abrupt Ozark hills on all sides. It had grown warmer, and we were looking for shade to have our usual morning snack. The large oak tree we spotted from a mile away had a mobile home near it, and a well-groomed lawn came right out to the pavement edge. We saw no one at the mobile, so we propped our bikes against the tree and sat down.

The three-wheel cycle came roaring down the road at us, as if the rider were intent upon confronting us as soon as possible. The older man riding the machine cornered sharply, slid into the driveway, and skidded to a stop beside us, increasing the uncomfortable feeling that we were probably parked on someone's lawn.

"Hello," he smiled, dismounting from the cycle and walking over. "I'm Charles Allen. This is my wife."

We had been so busy watching the cycle approach that we didn't notice the woman who had come out of the mobile home.

"Hello," I said, feeling a bit relieved. I introduced Lolly and Bill, and the five of us sat there on the lawn.

"We had a girl bicyclist through here one time," Mrs. Allen related. "We invited her in for lunch, and we had a great time. She promised she would write, but we never heard from her again."

I could sense Lolly's barely perceptible nod, and I knew how she feels about people who say they will do something and then don't do it.

"Have you been here a long time?" I asked.

Charles's look was on the melancholy side.

"Yes," he said. "We owned that ranch you see back there."

He gestured in a large semicircle, taking in everything on the one side of the road.

"Our kids have it now, and are running it."

"That's right," Mrs. Allen put in. "We've retired to our mobile home here, with only three acres to take care of. We're too old for working the farm."

"Do you like retirement?" I asked.

Oh, yes, they said. It was great. The lawn, all three acres of it, looked newly mown that very morning. A shiny riding mower stood near the mobile, every part wiped spotless after use. Not a blade of grass or a flower was out of alignment on the whole place. Even the road right-of-way had been mowed, right out to the pavement. Maybe he was too old to work the farm—but when things to do presented themselves, Charles Allen seemed eager to grasp them firmly, before they could escape.

Bendavis, Fairview and Houston were held apart only by that long, shoulderless, yo-yo ribbon of asphalt. We grumbled about the steep pitches, and I vowed never to go touring again without a lower set of gears for the bike. Lolly's knees were hurting most of the time now.

"Walt said to wait on you real slow so he can keep ahead," the waitress in Houston said laughingly. "You *are* the Skillmans, aren't you?"

We admitted it, and learned that Walt was about an hour ahead of us. Though we would have enjoyed his company, we knew he was beginning to get his second wind and was anxious to make better time. He would be able to make more mileage each day than we could, and we shared the unspoken feeling that Walt wanted to have his adventure alone. So did we; we had no thoughts of chasing after him.

The countryside became more wooded. We passed a state forest ranger station beside the road that boasted a fire lookout on a tall, skeletal steel tower. We climbed the steel and wood stairs to see treetops stretching miles to the horizon, the undulating surface a green carpet that changed into ever-lighter, fading hues of blues as the distance increased. There were many pines and lots of hardwood species mixed in the forest. I was just wishing I could recognize all the varieties when a fast-moving electrical storm approached. We got down off the tower in a hurry, the steps ringing metallically to our pounding descent.

We intended to camp where the Jacks Fork River, fifty feet wide and fast flowing, came up full-blown from a single huge spring in the limestone. Nearby campgrounds were closed and cordoned off with ropes and barricades warning of flash flood danger. Recent heavy rains, especially upstream, had made the water rise abruptly. The closed camps were a letdown for us; our energy was nearly spent in reaching that point. We thought about it awhile, and had an orange apiece before riding the 5 miles into Eminence over one of the steepest hills we had yet encountered.

Teresa Smith, smiling and energetic, was the waitress in the T & T restaurant in Eminence.

"I'm from Prineville, Oregon," she said, after learning where we lived. "My folks moved there when I was six. Just moved back here a few years ago. My husband and I cut blocks in the morning, and I waitress in the evening. We do all right."

We learned that blocks were short lengths of timber, usually hard-wood, used for making pallets.

"We cut on my father-in-law's land, so there's no trouble with the Forest Service or anything like that," she told us.

"Sounds like hard work," I said.

"Oh, no. My husband does the cutting. I just carry the blocks and load them on the truck."

Bill, Lolly and I looked at each other. Not hard work? I could just imagine heavy, green chunks of trees that needed to be dragged over and loaded on the truck. Teresa didn't look that strong, but there was an aura of the pioneer woman about her. I was reminded of other young people we knew who were hard workers.

We had seen hundreds of canoes stacked on racks at different places in Eminence, and painted signs that identified various outfitters who specialized in trips down the Current River. The river, at flood, was tempting no one today. We also noticed dozens of vehicles pulling horse trailers. A family with young children solved that mystery for us. They had come from Tennessee to take part in a five-day, 150-mile trail ride that began at Eminence.

Probably because we had come so far along our route, we were paying close attention to our daily average mileage, knowing that any unexpected delays like a particularly steep section of the country, or a fall, or really adverse weather could put us behind schedule so much that we wouldn't be able to complete the trip. The knee pain Lolly was suffering had become a factor. We had carefully adjusted the height of her bike seat and fitted the bike to her as well as we could. None of these things really helped much, and Lolly continued to experience considerable pain whenever we had hills to climb. Her independence made it difficult to convince her that I should be carrying more of our gear on my bike. Finally we compromised; she let me lighten her packs by a few pounds. To help all our knees, we began to pay more attention to the route ahead, trying to select detours that would avoid the worst hills. A chance meeting with a state patrolman in Ellington had convinced us to take country road HH as a shortcut to Piedmont, and had led us to Art Bowlby.

That evening in Piedmont, Bill and I de-gunked and cleaned the sprockets and chains on the bikes, and finally lubed them again. It may have been just imagination, but we thought we could detect a slight gain in efficiency.

As we rode east through Lutesville and Jackson on our way to the Mississippi, Bill began having shifting problems with his bike. We stopped at a bike shop in Cape Girardeau, where Bill bought a new chain, and we trued the rear wheel on Lolly's bike, which had been wobbling for days since hitting a huge chuckhole.

"Be careful riding over the river," the shop owner warned. "The bridge is narrow, and the cars will run you off the road. There's no place to go. Ride three abreast, and take the whole lane so they won't try to pass you on the bridge."

Reaching the Mississippi was an emotional experience, giving us a new perspective on the distance we had come so far. We stood on the bank a long time before crossing, taking pictures of the river and the ironwork of the old bridge. When we crossed, we did stay three abreast, pumping fast. The method worked well; only a few cars were behind us when we pulled off the road on the Illinois side, and none had tried to pass. At a nearby campground that night, Illinois formally welcomed us with rain showers and then settled down to make sure we weren't lacking for humidity.

It was getting dark when we rode into Elizabethtown, after a long day that included a backfiring shortcut. Flood waters had lifted away huge slabs of pavement, leaving a rough gravel surface. The shortcut had been recommended by a rider we met at breakfast that morning, and would have saved time and energy had it not been for the flood damage. As it was, the rough gravel pounded our bottoms and made us wish for pavement. The bikes survived, though, and carried us through Jonesboro, Boles, Vienna, Dixon Springs and Golconda. Golconda's huge surrounding dikes, cut only by narrow roadway openings fitted with slots for gateways, like locks at some dam, proclaimed something about life under siege from the river.

An hour before reaching Elizabethtown, I had noticed two people untying dogs in their yard adjacent to the road. They didn't know we were there, but the dogs sure did. Two of the animals came right out after us, and as usual Bill and I dropped back to keep the dogs busy while Lolly went on. The smaller dog gave up quickly, but the larger dog was serious. Bill managed to break away, and then it was just the dog and me. A bicycle pump weighs only a few ounces and is a poor weapon, but the dog doesn't know that. Every time the dog attacked, I managed to keep him from closing in by waving the pump and shouting. Then I would head the bike at the dog, who would run off the road as if disengaging, but the minute I turned to ride away, the dog would streak in again. This went on for several circles, and I grew angry. I knew I couldn't stop and put my feet down, because that brings your legs within easy reach of the dog and you can't maneuver while astraddle the bike. Soon the dog's owner was shouting at me instead of the dog, and things deteriorated rapidly. Breaking away finally, I could hear shouts behind me for a quarter of a mile.

Dog encounters were getting much more frequent, and the dogs more aggressive. Bites weren't the only concern; while concentrating on a dog you always face the danger of crashing on the bike or even being hit by a car. Lolly had thrown her water bottle at one dog. Bill had taken a swing at another with the tire pump, only to have the pump extend and catch in the rear spokes. Luckily, the light plastic pump disintegrated before the spokes were torn out. We started giving lots of thought to our dog problem.

That evening our main concern was finding a spot to stay in Elizabethtown. After riding nearly 90 miles that day, we had no desire to go any farther when we couldn't find a motel. It was getting darker by the minute. A local resident had no suggestions, but he did offer to take us to meet the local policeman. Following him, we saw some people standing in front of a small, white Baptist church.

"I'm Margaret Russell," the woman said. She had a friendly smile, and the lilt in her voice was sincere. "This is my husband Charles. And this is Ed Lafferty, our new pastor."

We introduced ourselves, and shortly Margaret was taking us on a tour of the church.

"I was raised here," she said. "My family has always been a part of this church."

Inside, the sanctuary fairly reeked with memories of the various families whose part in the church since 1887 came alive through Margaret's description. Outside, we looked more closely at the brick structure, now painted white.

"The bricks were made and fired right here, but they were soft," Margaret explained. "So we painted them to preserve the exterior walls."

Ed was restoring the parsonage, and was excited over finding rich, dark wood under the many coats of paint he was removing from the stairway and bannister. He thought it was black walnut.

"Sure you can camp on the lawn," the pastor agreed at my question. "Over by the side of the church is a good place. There's water at that hydrant."

It was already dark, and we needed flashlights to put up the tents. Dew was settling rapidly and with the quieting of darkness came thousands of fireflies, like tiny, elongated explosions of light, rising from the wet grass. We don't have fireflies in Oregon, and to see such a display was a real treat. Then we noticed that mosquitoes were assiduously hunting for a warm meal, and we retired to the tents. We talked a bit before going to sleep, about this interesting town that began as a freighting depot on the Ohio River, boomed briefly during World War II as a mining and shipping point, and now was diminishing. Like many of the small towns we had come through, it had lots of abandoned buildings, the commercial district was devastated, and many homes were either for sale or the owners had given up hope of a sale and abandoned them. Many of the residents were retired, and young people were forced to go elsewhere to find work. But Elizabethtown had the feeling of a river town, and about the time fatigue brought sleep, it was easy to imagine the thrilling blast of a steam whistle from some sternwheeler on the Ohio.

The throb of diesels in the little tug the next morning, shepherding the tiny eight-car ferry across the Ohio, sounded just right. Lolly had just bought a bag full of pastries from a Mennonite peddler who had his wagon parked at the main intersection, downtown Cave in Rock, while the horse was tethered down a side street. The one-dollar fare entitled us to ride off the ramp into Kentucky. We had some of the pastries right then, both because they looked good, and because the Pancake Postulate had come undone: now the farther east we rode, the smaller the pancakes in the cafes. Two stacks barely did the job.

We hadn't seen another cyclist for a week or more, so when two westbound riders came in sight, we stopped for a visit. They were young geologists, not long out of college, who had both quit jobs in order to go bicycle touring. They were en route to San Diego, they said proudly, and they had been making 35 miles a day. We talked awhile and then went on, wondering if this pair was going to make it. Their equipment was okay, but somehow they weren't talking like fellows who had the discipline to stay with it until they completed their ride. We didn't bother to tell them how long it would take at the rate they were going.

Not long after that, another pair of cyclists came into view. We learned that they were juniors in college, and they had been making 60 miles a day heading for the west coast. They questioned us on the route, and also had some queries on equipment and the way their bodies were adjusting to the routine of riding. Clearly they had the desire to make the ride, and they were apparently willing to back up that desire with sacrifice and hard work. We told them everything we could think of that might help, and wished them well. As we watched them pedal away, we couldn't help but notice the extra surge of power, prideful or maybe egotistical, that they applied to every turn of the pedals. Maybe this was for our benefit, to show us somehow that they were going to try. We each grinned, because these two seemed to have what it takes to make a long-distance ride.

That evening we camped in the city park in Sebree with five other cyclists who were on a group tour sponsored by Bikecentennial.

Part of the route ahead clearly went through mountains, so we had some decisions to make. At dinner we discussed searching out detours, even if they meant longer distances, to avoid as many steep hills as we could, at least until we got through the Appalachians. Of course, the choices were limited but we agreed to let Lolly select detours that would follow railroads or rivers, where the grades would be most likely to be gentle.

We also took a hard, Spartan look at the gear we were carrying, trying to figure out what we could get along without. Every pound we lightened the bikes would help; we were all beginning to understand this trade-off more clearly.

We turned southeast the next morning, following Lolly's navigation through Onton, Ashbyburg, Calhoun, Livermore, Hartford and Beaver Dam, places you would zip by in an automobile—provided you even travelled the secondary roads in the first place. In this area coal is the basis of a fluctuating economy, and the feel of the country and the attitude of the people was different. We couldn't put our finger on it, exactly, but an oppression sat on the countryside, much of which has been mined. At one place we stood, almost unbelieving, staring at a huge dragline used for strip mining that had a boom 150 feet long. Its bite was the size of our living room.

Strengthening our school-book impressions of Kentucky, we came upon an elderly farmer plowing his scraggly garden with a horse. A very modest house squatted under shade trees just beside the road. It was picturesque, and we pulled over to take photos. The farmer saw us, and stopped the horse to wave.

"You have a nice horse," Lolly called as the man walked up towards the fence.

"Thank you," the farmer responded.

"Your garden looks good," I put in, not knowing quite what to say.

"Well," the farmer hesitated, and then his look turned serious. "We have poor soil here. It isn't like the rich Illinois bottomlands. Have to keep after it to grow anything at all." He shook his head. "Poor soil."

"Thanks for letting us take your picture," Lolly said.

We mounted the bikes and rode on towards Leitchfield. When we were a long way down the road, I could see the farmer in my mirror, still standing by the fence looking towards us, and the horse still standing in the garden.

*June 16–June 19*

# 13

# IF RICHARD
# CAN DO IT

## LEITCHFIELD, KENTUCKY–PIPPA PASSES, KENTUCKY

The pancakes we ate in Leitchfield, Kentucky—in company with the publisher of the newspaper—were on the puny side, both in diameter and thickness, and in their ability to power straining bicyclists. Right after breakfast we stopped at the post office to mail home the items we'd sorted out from our gear. The post office had no cardboard boxes for sale, so I went into the newspaper office next door and asked the receptionist if they had any. The girl was busy talking to friends and drinking coffee, and she apparently didn't like my looks. No, they didn't have any boxes and from her attitude she conveyed that if they did, she wouldn't give them to me. No matter, a nearby auto-parts store let me pick through their selection.

We were packing the boxes in front of the post office when the editor of the paper came over. Having learned of us from her publisher, she wanted an interview, so we talked with her, and had our picture taken right in front of the newspaper office. Perhaps I enjoyed the situation too much, but I knew the receptionist inside could see us talking with the editor on the front lawn. Lolly asked if they would send us a copy of the story.

We were several pounds lighter when we left the post office. I had mailed a lot of exposed film for processing, and also sent an exposed roll to our local TV station at home. I rearranged the packs, and managed to talk Lolly into letting me take some of the small, heavy items she had been carrying.

But that was our only good experience with post offices that morning. No mail awaited us at our general delivery mail stop a few miles on in Sonora. We were all disappointed, but I felt especially sorry for Lolly, because she really looked forward to receiving the mail, and she was

# Riding Days 44-47
## 270.9 ROUTE MILES

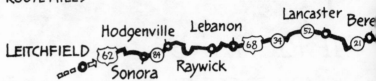

DANIEL BOONE
NAT'L FOREST

depressed for the remainder of the day. I put in a forwarding order in case the mail was only late in getting there.

"You can't sit there," the waitress in the huge truck-stop restaurant was saying.

I looked at the several empty booths along the window next to where we had just seated ourselves so we could see the bikes outside. No one was in any of them, and the restaurant had plenty of seating.

"The truck drivers sit here," the waitress said.

"They're not sitting here now," I pointed out.

"No, but if I let you sit here, one of them might see, and get mad." The girl looked flustered.

"Okay."

We moved to another area of the restaurant where, we were assured, no one would get mad at us. We couldn't see the bikes, but we had chained them securely to a signpost.

During lunch we discussed going to the Abraham Lincoln Birthplace National Historic Site, a spot we wanted to see even though it meant a round trip of several miles off our route through Hodgenville. The consensus was to ride the extra miles.

The beautiful marble shrine enclosing the cabin in which Lincoln was born was photogenic, especially with the wide granite steps leading up to it. Appearances would never give a clue that the structure was built in 1911. We walked around the grounds, and attended a movie put on by the Park Service in the headquarters building. The eighteen-minute film was interesting, but before it was over our fatigue level had us nodding.

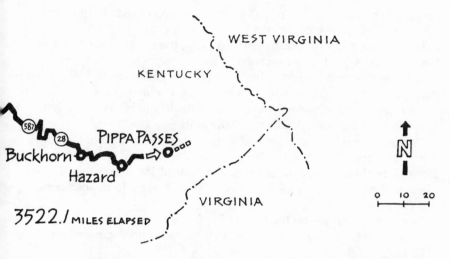

We were riding east through Raywick that afternoon, recognizing the edge of town by a cluster of buildings that looked like a gas-station-and-garage complex. As we rode by, several men were standing around a four-wheel Honda ATV near the gas pumps. We thought little of it, until a minute or two later we heard the machine start up, and roar out onto the road behind us. We didn't look back, but just kept on riding, not knowing what to expect but hearing the ATV gaining on us every second. Then the machine was beside us, and I looked over at the driver. He seemed to be growing out of the top of the ATV as though he had been crammed into a bucket. His face wore a wide smile, forecasting an outgoing personality. I realized the man had no legs.

We headed toward a wide spot on our side of the road, but the driver wasn't taking any chances. He gunned his machine ahead, pulled into the wide spot, and waved us over.

"I'm Richard Pile," he said. "Sort of a medical miracle."

"Hi, Richard." I introduced the three of us.

"A lot of bicyclists come through here," Richard said, gunning his motor in neutral for emphasis. "I talk with most of them."

"That's good. I'm glad we had a chance to meet you," I responded.

Richard obviously wanted to talk about his handicap. "It was cancer," he said. "I've lost my legs, and some of my lower spine and pelvis. Like I said, the doctors call me a medical miracle." His tone held no trace of resentment, and his personality bubbled.

"I bought this Honda," he went on, "and a friend helped with the modification. The doctors didn't see how I was going to manage, but I designed the whole thing myself. I can sit on top of the machine, and run all the controls with my hand."

He demonstrated for our benefit, working the clutch, gearshift and brakes with levers. It was functional if basic.

"I made this seat out of the bottom of a fifty-gallon drum," Richard admitted. "I just hoist myself up here on top, and away I go."

We commented admiringly on his handiwork, still not knowing how to respond to the open demeanor of the man.

"You see, I was an electrician and going to night school in engineering when the cancer got to me," Richard said. "So I know how to design things." He looked just the slightest bit wistful for a moment. "I get along fine now. The doctors don't know what is going to happen next, but I'm fine."

"You did a great job on the Honda," Lolly said.

"Yes," I said, "you can just sort of stuff yourself into that barrel seat."

Richard laughed.

"I'm not sensitive about it, as you can tell," he said. "I don't really know how much time I have left, but I do know one thing. I'm going to make the most of it."

The unreality of three hot and dirty bicyclists pulled over on a wide spot in the road in a little town in Kentucky talking about life and death with a legless man who sat in a barrel on top of a four-wheel Honda sent prickles through me. Richard went on as if he had known us for years.

"A lot of people tighten up when I meet them," Richard said. "I got over that a long time ago. I'm just going to go on living."

"Looks like you're doing a pretty good job of it," Bill observed.

"Well, I have to go back for some more tests soon," Richard said. "When that's over with, I want to go back to college and finish my engineering degree. I've just got a little left to finish. After that, we'll see."

"You're pretty strong, Richard," I said.

"Why not?" he asked. "It wouldn't do any good to feel sorry for myself. So I put everything I can into life."

We learned that Richard shared his strength with others, too. He received mail from all over, and always answered those who had written him seeking help in handling their physical problems. Richard seemed able to pass his positive attitude on to others. Two local women, both cancer victims, had sought him out just to talk, and his continuing support had helped them to make the most of their condition, just as Richard was doing. He would tell his nephews and others that their strength lay inside themselves. As he told us about his challenges and why he kept going, we believed it.

"You can finish your degree if you decide to," Lolly said.

"Sure," Richard said.

Then he gave us some suggestions about the route into Lebanon, where we intended to stay the night. The Honda's engine revved.

"Good-bye," Lolly called. "It's been an inspiration meeting you."

Richard spun the Honda around sharply, straightened it and waved. We watched silently as the man with no legs roared off up the street. Suddenly, we weren't tired, and we didn't hurt. If Richard could live life with such enthusiasm, what were we doing complaining about a few hills?

Richard Pile died in January 1987.

For two days we rode through the Kentucky countryside, where small farms depended upon corn, beans, and occasionally a patch of tobacco. Drying barns for the tobacco crop were everywhere, but most were not in use. Occasionally, a horse farm set on a scenic knoll would impress us with beautiful serpentine approaches flanked by white board fences. The people we met were friendly and helpful.

Near Lancaster, miles of stone fences give the countryside the flavor of England. Limestone chunks, stacked flat and topped by slabs set on edge, sneak like gray ribbons over the undulating hills. Huge, wide barns dot the fields; in June scattered oaks generously sprinkle shade everywhere but on the road.

The pavement was narrow, and shoulders nonexistent. The right lane could not hold us and a car simultaneously; on curves this meant either that we jolted off into the grass, or the car slowed and followed until the way was clear.

We are wearing down. The constant riding without rest has depleted our reserves. We promise ourselves that tomorrow, or the next day, we will either take a layover day, or ride for only a half day. But it doesn't happen. Lolly calculates that we still have over 1,000 miles to go on the route. Neither Bill nor I have stopped to add it up, but when we look at the map, we are nowhere near the Atlantic, and it is already past the middle of June.

Somewhere in this section, I become lax in warning of stops, and Lolly, watching for traffic behind and as vulnerable as ever, nearly crashes into Bill when we both stop suddenly. Fatigue has shortened tempers, and I get a sound chewing and, for a while, the silent treatment. I can't blame Lolly; never throughout the trip has she wavered in watching for traffic behind.

About an hour before reaching Berea, Bill points out a low mountain ridge on the horizon ahead. This is the beginning of the Appalachian

Mountains. We've heard conflicting reports about the area, and we don't know what to expect.

Our approach to the Appalachians led us into the mountains in disarmingly gentle fashion. A lightly travelled, two-lane road meandered up a narrow valley on a grade barely discernible to our knees. Following a watercourse, we twisted along with the road through green fields and patches of woods until we looked more closely at the map. On paper at least, our road appeared to lead up the valley for a number of miles before heading back towards us on the other side of the stream we had been following. In fact, the return portion was within a mile of where we stood looking at our map. The dirt road that led invitingly across the stream on an old bridge beckoned so convincingly with promise of miles saved that we could not resist, and in minutes we had ridden along the faint track through two backyards where dogs barked and growled at us menacingly. The 10-mile savings was more than worth it.

Shoulders on the road were still nonexistent, which meant we were riding at the extreme right edge of the traffic lane, in direct interaction with the local traffic. Most drivers moved over for us, passing with wide clearance. Others, behind us on the frequent sharp, blind corners, slowed abruptly to our speed, followed us around and then gunned their engines and spurted by. Black rubber skid marks on the pavement provided graphic evidence of the habits of the poorer drivers and it was hard to keep from flinching when a powerful engine came within hearing, accompanied by the shrill complaint of rubber on asphalt. But ordinary cars and pickups were tame compared to the coal trucks.

Visualize a tall, wide, long box on ten or fourteen big wheels. Now add a snarling diesel engine with an exhaust on the right side jetting out a powerful stream of black smoke at navel height. Stir in driver determination fueled by pay based on the number of trips driven during a given time period. You are staring at a coal truck.

Make the vehicle the width of one lane on a two-lane country road, so there will be barely enough room for two to pass, and you will begin to understand the fear that crunches a cyclist's innards when he hears the roar of its engine. So paranoid about coal trucks did we become that when B-52 bombers practiced low-level intrusion flights in the area we found ourselves diving for the grass roadside, only to grin sheepishly at each other when we realized that the roar wasn't a coal truck.

Several times we were on the road at a point that coincided with the passing of two coal trucks going opposite directions. There was no chance or thought of staying anywhere near the pavement; we just rode off into the grass and hoped for the best. To their credit, nearly all the coal truck drivers were entirely courteous. If we were unable to pull off the road, they would gear down and stay behind us. It was obvious, as is often the case when drivers own their vehicles, that they were highly skilled in maneuvering them.

We were dismayed at the way the Appalachians affected us. Of all the areas we had ridden through, this was the first in which we felt a strong negative impact. The friendliness other areas had taught us to expect was lacking here. Dirt, squalor and poverty were apparent everywhere we looked. But most depressing of all was the people's acceptance of the circumstances of their lives. We would wave and call to families sitting on their porches, and sometimes they would wave or return our greeting. Many times, however, our hail went unanswered. As often as not, wide, blank eyes stared at us, sometimes with transparent resentment.

More garbage littered the roadsides the deeper we penetrated into the mountains. Every wide spot became a dump. We could see garbage and smell garbage all the time. Some banks beside the road became miniature avalanche chutes, conveying old appliances, cars, tires and all sorts of discarded goods downwards into the brush-covered ravines below.

Many dogs came out at us. When a particularly intent animal charged resolutely at her, Lolly had a chance to try the pressure can of repellant that I had bought for her in Berea. Engulfed in a cloud of cayenne pepper from the squirt can, the dog halted suddenly as if reaching the end of a leash, and without a sound, slunk away. Immediately Lolly's confidence in completing the ride without dog bite soared.

But Appalachia's strongest aura was the despair of its people. Poverty is one thing, but when members of a society give up hope or the desire to make life better, it is a terrible thing to witness. One family in particular, sitting on their porch at arm's length from the road, exemplified the presence we felt. The very young children stared at us expressionless, no spark of interest or curiosity in their wide, brown eyes. A teenager gave us a look of resentment and apparent rage, but at least his face conveyed enough emotion to confirm that he had seen us. The stares of the older folks were empty, going right through us to the brushy hillside behind; not even their heads moved to watch us ride by. As far as they were concerned, we did not exist, nor did the world from which we came. What social standard accepts an environment where babies and children can grow up without hope?

Coal and the way it is procured may have a lot to do with the attitudes we found in this section of Kentucky. Certainly coal is the basis of that wildly fluctuating economy; without the influx of jobs and resources provided by the fossil fuel, families would have little income. We saw no agriculture worth mentioning, and in the very rural area through which we were riding, no other industry to support population.

The rolling hills, low but steep, were covered solidly with undergrowth and hardwoods. A short way down the road a very young mother, with a baby in frequently laundered but clean clothing, waved and smiled.

Buckhorn, Kentucky, is more than a wide spot where two roads come together and local folks go to get their groceries. Two things make it more, and one of them is H. C. Sharp. H. C. runs the general store, and supplies the neighbors with most everything they need for local shopping. We stopped in to get a snack and talk with the storekeeper.

"My grandfather started the store," H. C. told us.

He noticed me looking at the large number of account books on the shelf.

"Yes, a lot of my business is on the cuff," he smiled. "People need to eat whether they are working or not. When they can, they pay. I haven't lost much over the years."

Wandering around the store looking at merchandise, we could tell the store was more than a place to buy things. One man entered and asked H. C.'s advice on a business matter. A woman, asking about the merits of some food items, stocked up with groceries. It was evident that the word of H. C. Sharp carried influence and respect in Buckhorn. In a community where the golden rule still functions, the little center of commerce that H. C.'s grandfather started is not only doing well today, but providing service.

A large church across the road, made of sawn planks whose strength and permanence contrasted strikingly with most of the construction thereabouts, drew us like a magnet. We found the Presbyterian men and women sorting donated clothing in preparation for a rummage sale to be held in a hall to the rear of the forty-foot-tall church.

One of the church ladies approached us. "Would you like to see the organ?"

"We sure would," Lolly affirmed. She introduced the three of us.

We followed the woman inside, struck by the simple design of the huge timber arches supporting the glowing, oaken ceiling high above. Wood was obviously the available material, and oak planks and boards were what the church was built from, massive amounts of oak that gave off a gray and golden feeling of solidity and peace. At one end of the building stood a huge pipe organ.

"We had the organ rebuilt recently," the woman told us. "There are only a few people left who can repair the old pipe organs."

We could imagine the resonance of those huge pipes assailing the congregation members on Sunday, filling the building with sound. The graduated tubes of the organ reached far up the front wall, spread out like rays of a vertical fan.

"We need to get the exterminator out again," the woman observed. "We have lots of trouble with the bats. We really do have bats in the belfry, plenty of them. We've had them exterminated several times, but they keep coming back."

Bill looked up, and you could tell his mind was thinking about more than the beautiful oaken structural arches.

"Try high frequency sound," he said.

The woman seemed interested, but we didn't know if she understood that bats navigate with sonar. Someday we may learn if the Presbyterian Church in Buckhorn, Kentucky, has rid itself of bats.

The four approaching cyclists looked to us much as we must have looked to them, except our hair had some gray in it while these were obviously young people. When we got closer, we could identify one girl and three fellows, helmeted and wearing the gear of serious touring riders. They obviously wanted to talk, so we pulled together into a wide spot just off the road. A more enthusiastic group you could not imagine, and it was plain that the beaming smiles and desire to tell someone about their experiences stemmed from their success so far. Yet we could detect an uncertainty also, an underlying doubt about something. "I'm Lynn Finnegan," the girl said, as we introduced ourselves.

We also met Clay Hightower, and two of his friends. They were from the Atlanta area, and had begun their ride not far from where we intended, God willing, to end ours, and were headed for the Pacific Coast.

The discussion centered on the roller-coaster road, and on the hot weather, and on places to stay and eat.

"Does your bottom hurt?" I overheard Lynn asking Lolly.

"Yes, that's one thing that doesn't seem to get in shape like the rest of me," Lolly laughed. "You may get used to spending eight or ten hours on that seat, but I haven't."

We learned that the three boys were going back to college at the end of the summer after they finished their ride. Lynn was going to work as a secretary for a judge in Tallahassee. We wished each other well, and as they rode away, Lolly and I looked at each other. These were good young people, the kind we had hoped to meet and perhaps help in some way. Had we given them any inspiration? Lolly smiled. The way those kids kept looking at us and at our equipment, and the way they soaked up information we gave them put their thoughts on their foreheads in neon: "If these old people can do it, we sure can!"

Our American Youth Hostel listing showed lodgings run by Ed and Charlotte Madden in Pippa Passes. The village nestles in a narrow canyon at the bottom of a hill so steep it seemed we would fall over the handlebars. In minutes we were stripped of the elevation it had taken the better part of an hour to gain. Houses nudged each other for room close on each side of the road as we coasted into the center of the village, where the local policeman took time out from his duties on a shady porch to point the way to the hostel. I had phoned the Maddens for reservations. We were supposed to go right in and make ourselves comfortable because they wouldn't be back until late.

It felt strange to walk into someone else's home. At first we weren't sure that the large, two-story house at the edge of the trees a couple of blocks up a steep, knee-tearing hill from the main drag was the right place. We decided it was, and after determining which rooms were used for hostel purposes, claimed three beds. There wasn't a whole lot of conversation that evening, because the beds were good and the ride had been long and tiring. We didn't hear Ed or Charlotte come in.

At their insistence the next morning, we had toast and homemade jelly with the Maddens. We learned that Ed was an administrator in education, while Charlotte had just retired as librarian from Alice Lloyd College, an institution that dwarfs the remainder of the village of Pippa Passes. Both run the hostel because they like people and enjoy the variety of folks who stay with them. We showered, and then Bill and Lolly re-packed some gear while I stayed put long enough to write the column. I knew that the editor receiving it would look long and hard at the postmark: Pippa Passes, Kentucky.

Our location on the map was beginning to look pretty good to us, especially on a map of the entire United States. A lot more land lay to the west of us than stretched ahead to the east. Most of the ride was behind us; Lolly's navigation indicated that we had come over 3,500 miles in forty-seven days of constant riding. The pace was wearing on us, and we talked about laying over for a half day. The idea of not riding for one glorious day, or even a half day, was delicious contemplation. But what if we did stop, and then after that some mechanical failure or sickness unexpectedly cost us a day or two? What then? We didn't seem to be losing too much weight, we were still strong—and insomnia was not a problem.

# 14 
# *FATIGUE*

PIPPA PASSES, KENTUCKY–MONTICELLO, VIRGINIA

Riding the route east of Pippa Passes was like being on a stationary bicycle in the middle of one large garbage dump. Perhaps there is no place to get rid of the flotsam and jetsam of modern conveniences, food and consumer goods, but in this section of the Appalachians one has just to look, and everything that has been purchased and either partially eaten, worn out or broken is sitting by the side of the road or thrown over an embankment. The smell permeated the countryside.

My recollection is one kaleidoscope of coal trucks and unfriendly stares. We were not welcome here, apparently contrasting too much with the lives of the local people or at least with the way they perceive their lives and are apparently content to live them. So we stayed on the road, minded our own business, and pedaled to put this section of the country behind us as soon as possible. Places like Dema, Bevinsville, Bypro, Melvin, Virgie, Pound River and Elkhorn City struggle bravely, and provide local centers for the people, but we just wanted to get through them without having things thrown at us, or suffering dog bites.

And dogs are everywhere, hounds, spaniels, beagles; what surprised us most were the number of Dobermans used for watchdogs. Most of the animals are chained to their houses and apparently stay that way, wearing the poor soil down to a poorer subsoil and in some cases right down to bare rock. Twice we noticed wolves in pens.

Road-killed animals are left where they fall, often flattened and run over repeatedly. The stench of their rotting flesh was never far away.

June 21 was our thirty-third wedding anniversary, and though this wasn't exactly my idea of the ideal environment in which to celebrate, we couldn't do much about that. The area we rode through in the afternoon was only lightly populated, but we did find a motel with a swimming pool just across the line in Virginia. Part of the celebration was that we would get to stop early.

# Riding Days 48-53
## 383 ROUTE MILES

KENTUCKY | WEST VIRGINIA

Bevinsville
Elkhorn
City
PIPPA PASSES
122
80
Haysi
460
Bluefield
19
460
Claypool Hill

"Sure we have a room," the motel manager said. "But stay out of the adjoining room. The door between was broken by a jealous husband."

Sure enough, the door connecting our room and the empty room adjacent hung partly open, out of line with its splintered jamb. We shrugged it off, and went swimming. There was a cafe and general store across the road, so we went over and had a fried-chicken dinner. Lolly was carrying a small packet, which she gave to me along with an anniversary card. In the packet was a tiny gold tie pin in the shape of a bicycle. The miniature wheels turned, and there was even a taillight made of a tiny ruby. She had designed the pin and had it made before we left home, carrying it in her pannier three-quarters of the way across the United States. Then I gave her a card, and a new bike jersey I had seen in a shop a few hundred miles back. We both agreed that of the many places we have spent our special anniversary day, this was one of the strangest.

After dinner we wandered through the store. Large signs entreated us: "SEE THE LIVE SNAKES," while arrows pointed the way. Lolly grimaced. Neither of us had any desire to visit what was evidently a popular local attraction.

We rode only 49 miles the next day, our shortest mileage since the snowstorm in Idaho. The fatigue that forty-nine days of marathon-style riding had induced was making it harder to ride our usual 75-mile day. Our bodies weren't bouncing back the way they had at the beginning of the trip, ready for more riding each morning. The riding itself didn't seem harder, it was just that when we stopped it took more will power to climb back on the bikes. The hard pedaling against the wind for many weeks had taken its toll. We. searched the map carefully, trying to

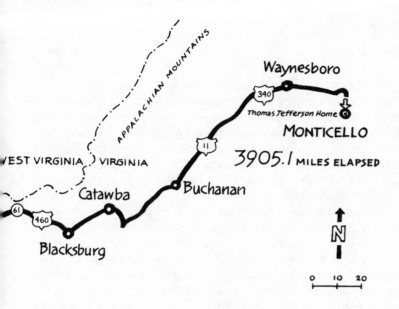

Waynesboro

340

Thomas Jefferson Home

MONTICELLO

3905.1 MILES ELAPSED

11

APPALACHIAN MOUNTAINS

WEST VIRGINIA  VIRGINIA

Catawba

Buchanan

61

460

Blacksburg

N

0    10    20

identify steep hills and so avoid them by detours if possible. As it turned out, we were successful in doing just that several times, but usually at the cost of additional miles ridden.

Our equipment was holding up better than we were. Aside from the fact that our bikes were dirty, and our panniers a little more worn, you wouldn't have known that we had come most of the way across the country. True, the brilliant, fluorescent orange stuff bags protecting our sleeping bags had long ago mellowed into a subdued hue but still, in spite of that, provided good visibility. Aluminum bottle racks had chafed black contact rings around our water bottles. And our shoes, in spite of the washing they received each time it rained, looked grubby. Where our jerseys and shorts ended a permanent-looking tan began. Even the web pattern on the back of our riding gloves was burned into our hands.

As our route led into more populated country, the amount of traffic picked up. We noticed that our presence on the road was of little concern to drivers here; when there was no ridable shoulder and we were limited to the few inches of outside, right-hand pavement, we knew that to waver would invite being hit. Luckily, the loaded bikes had become a part of us, and riding straight and predictably had become second nature. But these conditions do not favor enjoyment of a ride through the countryside.

Bluefield welcomed us with a sign boasting some of the best weather in that region and if they were wrong and the temperature went over ninety degrees, free lemonade was the cure. According to the sign, it had been nearly three years since any free lemonade flowed in Blue-field. We were more interested in getting lunch, and asked directions to a place that had a good salad bar. Again we were amazed at a characteristic of many Easterners: ignorance of what is on the other side of town. Being from the west coast, where nearly everyone is quite mobile and has been many places, we were always puzzled by this phenomenon. Maybe, because things are so good for Easterners, they have no need or desire to explore what exists around them.

The cafe we finally found was partly a bar, and not busy this Sunday morning. We had become complacent about leaving our bikes and panniers outside whenever we stopped for food or to shop, probably because nothing had ever been touched. We were in the middle of steak sandwiches when Lolly, who was sitting facing the outside where the bikes were, gave a startled exclamation. Bill and I turned quickly and saw a flash of movement through the window, in the area where our bikes were. Both of us jumped up and Bill beat me to the front door.

"What's going on here?" Bill hollered as he swung down onto the sidewalk outside. I was right behind him, trying to assess the situation; two younger men in riding clothes were stepping out of the area where our bikes were chained. I was trying to keep an eye on them and look our bikes and panniers over at the same time.

"What do you mean?" one of the men asked.

I was just beginning to tell myself that the two looked tough, and maybe this wouldn't be easy, when it dawned on both Bill and me that now two more bikes stood next to ours. These fellows had merely decided that where our bikes were chained was a good place to put theirs.

Just then they realized how their nearness to our bikes must have looked through the high windows of the cafe, and we all had a good laugh. We learned that they were from a nearby town, and had ridden over to Bluefield for lunch. We went back into the cafe and finished eating, while the other two riders sat at an adjoining table. They told us they had been startled to see us fly out the door at them. It was hours before our jolt of adrenaline wore off, and the experience served to make us realize how dependent we actually were on our bikes and equipment.

One thing made necessary by fatigue was to do our best not to let things bother or upset us. That evening I had a flat tire just as we were riding over to a fast-food place that had an excellent salad bar, and fixing it delayed us for fifteen minutes. We were hungry, and when we got there, the place was packed. We filled our plates and then went back for seconds while everyone in the establishment stared at us. Some of those staring were wearing shorts too.

"When I get home," Lolly said, "I'm going to spend a lot of time going to cafes and staring at people."

Over the many weeks we had grown accustomed to standing out, but the reaction we caused in Appalachia was different from the interested stares of the curious, friendly people we had met so far, and we were beginning to resent and even get a little testy about it. Maybe it was the hot, humid weather. To add to the aggravation of the evening, on the way back to our motel, the same tire on my bike went flat again.

Traffic continued to increase as we proceeded eastward. We continually looked forward to country roads and light traffic and a rest from the constant procession of cars. Only rarely was there a shoulder to ride on, whether the road was a heavily used main route or a meandering byway, so riding enjoyment was directly proportional to how light the traffic was. But now we found very few lightly travelled routes. I don't know if the miles we had ridden dulled our fear of traffic roaring by close beside us, or if fatigue caused us to care less, but the result was that we were able to ride under conditions that, had they been encountered at the beginning of the trip, might have caused us to quit. No friendly waves here; just a swerve or a honk to let us know that we weren't appreciated for taking up even our tiny slice of the roadway.

A couple of weeks previously, I had noticed loose bearings on my bike's crank set that were telegraphed by a wobble in the pedals and a crunching sound as they revolved. We had lacked the proper spanner wrench to adjust the bearings, so Bill took a screwdriver and using a rock, loosened the lock ring, adjusted the bearings, and locked the ring again. But I could tell that things weren't right with those bearings; they had probably been damaged by riding too far and too hard while they were loose. So, as we rode into Blacksburg and I noticed we were passing a bike shop, I pulled in.

Mike Matzuk, the owner of the East Coasters Bike Shop became very interested when he saw an Ashland, Oregon, sticker on the bikes.

"My wife Tana was born in Ashland," he said.

"Really?" I introduced Lolly and Bill, and thought about how our collection of "small world" incidents had grown. Then we began to talk about people we both knew. Before long Tana came in and joined us in recalling places and people she had grown up with.

"My parents still live in Ashland," Tana said. "I've been away for ten years, but I still love it there."

"We were interested in a bike shop near Ashland," Mike said. "We were going to buy it, but couldn't agree on everything. So we ended up here."

We talked while Mike installed new bearings.

"By the way," Mike said, "I passed you down the highway as I drove to work this morning. You were wobbling around quite a bit."

Our wobbling slightly to get a little more room when traffic was too close had become a habit, and we did it without thinking.

"Did that make you steer out around us?" I asked.

"Yes, I guess it did," Mike said.

"There's no shoulder on that road, just a four-inch-wide white line on the right side. If I appear to wobble, the traffic gives us more room."

Mike thought about that awhile, and I couldn't tell if he approved or not. The technique worked for us, but we were careful not to overdo it, to make it only a slight wobble, and always to watch and see if the overtaking traffic was actually going to move over. To an experienced rider like Mike, the maneuver would probably be misinterpreted, but still effective.

From Blacksburg, our route led eastward along the north fork of the Roanoke River and what was, to us, the prettiest part of the trip east of the Rockies. Homes were spread over the small valley, many of them obviously the headquarters for small farms. Others declared by their appearance that they had been there for a long time, and the atmosphere held a promise of pleasant living. I'm sure residents of that valley don't want it to change.

A mail snafu had plagued us since Colorado, with something always preventing us from receiving our mail at each scheduled stop. Now we planned to pick up our mail in care of general delivery in Buchanan, and hurried through the small towns of Catawba and Troutville to get to Buchanan before the post office closed. When it became apparent that we couldn't make it, I called the police department in Buchanan to see if they would pick it up for us. They said the mail would be waiting for us in Jane's Kitchen. It wasn't.

Jane's was a bustling spot, one of those places where all the local people gather at all hours of the day to learn all there is to know that they don't already know about everybody. I asked the waitress about the mail and got nothing but a blank stare. Either the police dispatcher had mislaid our request, or the postmaster had refused to give up our mail, but the result was the same. So we looked over the menu and decided that we might as well eat right there.

A man the waitress called Carl came out of the kitchen to take our order. That he was a real character was evident from the banter in the kitchen and among the other customers. We didn't know exactly what we wanted to order but it didn't matter. At our hesitation, Carl began to tell us what was the best eating.

"You seem to know a lot about the food," I said.

"I should," he said, "because I own the place, and I do a lot of cooking and waiting on tables."

About that time I noticed he was wearing a gun in his belt.

"Why the gun?" Bill asked.

He grinned, as if he had been waiting for that one.

"The food's so bad I have to force people to eat it." He didn't quite keep a straight face, as he sat down at the table with us.

We learned that he was a sergeant in the local police force, the person who would have picked up our mail had everything gone well. "The postmaster will have your mail first thing in the morning," he said by way of apology.

All during his conversation with us he was keeping up with the patter in the kitchen and among the customers, not missing a beat or a chance for a wisecrack, and answering questions from his friends. It became apparent that besides the cafe and the police job, Carl worked another eight hours a day. The cafe had been destroyed when the river flooded, and it had taken him a lot of time to repair the damage. We nodded as he told us about the flood, because we had seen many signs of high water.

When the food came, it lived up to the billing. If our sergeant friend had a hand in the cooking, it was a skilled one. A customer at another table told us that all the work in the cafe and police department had brought on a heart condition. It was not hard to imagine, watching the sergeant joking with customers one minute, rushing here and there the next, and always with that little police radio nearby so he could respond to whatever the community called upon him to do. It was obvious that Jane's Kitchen ran so well and was so popular because he had a hand in making it work that way.

"I'll bet I can knock on the door of the post office and get the mail early," Lolly said about seven the next morning.

"I doubt it," I replied. "Government employees, you know."

Lolly was back about seven-thirty from the short ride to the post office, all smiles, even though it was raining hard. She had a half ton of mail, which included everything from the prior two aborted stops. We looked for a place to open it where we would be out of the rain.

"Maybe they'll let us have a corner table in Jane's," Lolly said.

The waitress smiled and waved us to a clean table, where we fairly tore open letters and packages. There were cookies from a friend, and a delicious cake from Cindy. We had cards and messages from friends who had been following our column back home. The look on Lolly's face was evidence that the U.S. Postal Service was back in good graces.

Vesuvius is a good name for a crossroads where the transcontinental route climbs up sharply to follow the Blue Ridge Parkway. It is also the spot where, if your knees hurt, you look at your map and find another route that takes you to the same place without climbing any more mountains than necessary. Lolly's knees hurt a lot, so we adjusted our heading and visited Waynesboro, where a manager of the Red Carpet Inn must have been a bike rider himself, because he found us a nice room in what otherwise was a "full" motel.

Monticello, the home of Thomas Jefferson, had been beckoning us for weeks and had become a sort of milestone along the way. We calculated that if we could just put two 80-mile days back to back, we would have time to visit the home. We did that, but the ride into Charlottesville on Highway 250 was frantic; narrow pavement, no shoulder and lots of traffic. At least we had no trouble following road signs out of town to the famous spot.

"Lock your bikes to the fence right there where I can watch them," the fellow overseeing bus loading at Monticello told us. "Take what you want with you, and I'll see that the rest is okay while you're gone."

The ride up the hill to the estate in a small diesel-powered bus was exhilarating after so much pedaling. We hadn't been in a powered vehicle since the ride to a laundromat in Wyoming. Then we were inside Monticello, wandering back through time, aware that history books read long ago didn't quite get their points across. The tour of Monticello brought about a feeling that seemed half awe and half awareness of things great and past. The visit there was more than enjoyable, it was one of those experiences that affect me by making the hair on the back of my neck stand up. A certain flavor of the man is apparent in many of Thomas Jefferson's innovations around the place, and I thought that if somehow Thomas Jefferson were alive today, besides his other accomplishments he probably would ride a bicycle.

Monticello sits on a high hill, and from the elevated site of the mansion we could look eastward and see the Piedmont Plains, a fan of alluvium that appeared to stretch all the way to the Atlantic. From our vantage point, it was a smooth surface carpeted with trees, dipping ever so slightly as it progressed eastward. The expanse faded into the ever-paler blues of distance, giving a promise of easier riding that was not overlooked. We stood there for a long time, discussing the panorama in front of us, and letting our feelings sort themselves out. Now that we had reached Monticello after talking about it for days, what was next?

The country ahead looked to be solid forest, and maybe, just maybe, the traffic would be less. As we watched, a plume of smoke arose from a fire far out in the distance, proclaiming that the Piedmont Plain was certainly inhabited and not some pristine area through which we could ride without being affected. One thing seemed apparent; no more mountains stood between us and our goal.

# 15 ♟♟♟

# *THE ATLANTIC*

## MONTICELLO, VIRGINIA—VIRGINIA BEACH, VIRGINIA

Something's wrong, I thought. I was encircling my lower thigh with both hands, and my fingers overlapped. A few weeks ago this part of my leg had been much larger, impossible to reach around, swelled by muscles developed from pedaling and ready to power my bike anywhere I wished. Now, from the continuous, day-after-day riding without recuperative rest, those muscles were shrinking. If our goal of completing the ride within sixty days seemed within reach, it was because we had pushed ourselves physically against time and hills and nearly constant headwinds to make it so. We were paying the price.

Rest seemed an elusive thing. We would get to bed as soon as possible after finding a place to stay, eating, doing our laundry and writing in our logs, and had no trouble falling asleep almost instantly. But upon arising in the morning I didn't feel rested. My muscles didn't feel sore in the usual sense; my entire body just felt secondhand—used. We didn't talk about it, but each of us was aware of the increasing fatigue level, and I'm sure we each measured off our reserves against the remaining distance on a day-to-day basis in our minds. The stresses on us were increasing.

The little town of Fork Union, Virginia, seemed a good place to hole up for the night and plan the safest route through the traffic around Richmond. For several days riding conditions had been growing worse. The increased population as we approached the east coast was only part of it; the most noticeable thing to us was that the roads, carrying an ever-heavier traffic load as we neared the metropolitan areas, weren't much wider. Heavy traffic has never been noted for improving the disposition of drivers, either, and we felt a definite resentment, worse than in Appalachia, on the part of many a motorist at our mere presence on the roadway. Manifested in swerving close to us at high speeds, the motorists' unconcern had us really concerned. It was not unusual for a car to pass within a foot of our left handlebar and pannier at 60 miles an hour,

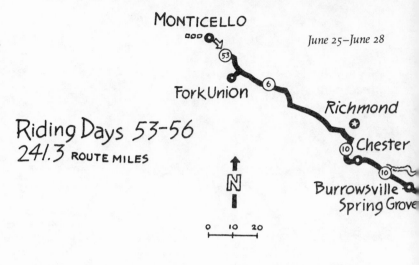

Riding Days 53-56
241.3 ROUTE MILES

N

0    10   20

VIRGINIA
— · — · — · — · — · — · — · — · — · — · — · — · —
NORTH CAROLINA

seemingly always in a place where severe drop-offs or guard rails gave us no escape from the road. Maybe the drivers really felt no malice; maybe conditions do require that they hurry and crowd and compete.

Some stretches of the countryside were downright beautiful, like scenes from *Gone With the Wind*. Stately groves of oaks that appear to date from the beginning of time provide shade and frame for plantation-style mansions. Ornate gate posts, some of them masterpieces of brick or stone in themselves, guard long, sweeping driveways that set off structures and groves with sweeping approaches, compelling the eyes to look and to see. In these areas, we took advantage of country roads to keep the traffic at bay.

Lolly, always the dependable rear guard, at first tried to keep us informed of traffic from the rear. She was constantly calling out "Car! . . . Car!" as the traffic became too thick to separate.

"I'm not going to call cars anymore," Lolly shouted ahead over the roar of tires and engines along the highway. "There are too many of them."

"Okay!" Bill and I shouted simultaneously. Lolly had done an excellent job.

Shortly after that, in a small town, two trucks like road-maintenance vehicles rumbled by. Both had low wooden cages, not more than four feet high, on the middle of the truck bed, and in those cages, staring out into the blinding sun, were men. I could hardly believe what I was seeing. Then I remembered that there were several prisons in the area, and I realized the trucks hauled some sort of work detail. Still, the image

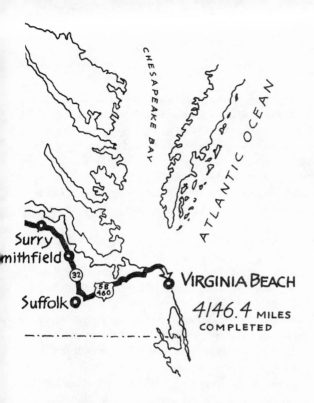

CHESAPEAKE BAY

ATLANTIC OCEAN

Surry

Smithfield

Suffolk

32

58
460

VIRGINIA BEACH

*4146.4* MILES
COMPLETED

of those faces, staring out through the wooden planks from the backs of trucks on a humid day in the nineties, shook me.

The roads led us by many points of historical interest, including Civil War bivouacs. Accustomed to country in the west that has been blessed with modern settlement for only 130 years, we could barely grasp the age of places two and three hundred years old. A high point was the Hope Merchant Church, dating back to the mid-1600's. Place names took on historical authority, and as we rode over a bridge spanning the James River, we found ourselves grinning for no apparent reason. The river was wide, and we were quite ready to believe that its flow at that point was affected by tidewater.

It wasn't our plan to ride during the 4:00 to 6:00 PM rush hour, but we found ourselves south of Richmond and very much caught up in the flow. Nothing at that moment sounded as good as finding a nice motel where we could get out of the traffic and rest awhile.

We made it to Chester and gave up for the day. We had ridden only 71 miles, but it had been one of the most tiring days so far. Dealing with the traffic was getting to us mentally. So much so that when Lolly found a barber shop open in town, Bill and I showed a remarkable lack of enthusiasm. But finally, realizing that the end of the trip was not far away and that we badly needed trimming, we obediently walked over to the shop. Soon, all three of us felt lighter and much cooler.

Getting up early seemed like a good plan; we wanted to clear the Richmond traffic before it became too heavy. But this didn't work. Maybe the traffic goes on all around the clock, or maybe the plants around Hopewell stagger their shift hours to alleviate traffic jams at shift changes. Regardless, the net result was that we were riding in heavy traffic in the early morning for 10 miles. Finally, in the area of Burrowsville, Cabin Point and Spring Grove, we had a respite: the road amazingly sprouted a two-foot-wide shoulder. We congratulated ourselves on our good luck.

In the middle of those congratulations, something happened that made us catch our breath—literally. A huge livestock truck, coming from behind, passed and engulfed us in a humid, strangling odor that nearly knocked us from the bikes. We were climbing a grade at the time, our lungs filtering large quantities of air for whatever oxygen was left in the stuff, and we could do nothing but continue to pant. In a crosswind we could have held our breath until the wind blew the stench to the side of the road. As usual we had a headwind, and it was minutes before the sickly odor diminished. Its source was plain to anyone raised in the country. Even before we saw a round, pink snout sticking out a ventilation hole in the side of the truck, we knew we were being assailed by a truckload of hogs. In the course of an hour, several more trucks loaded with pigs went by.

"SURRY HOUSE RESTAURANT," the sign proclaimed, and since it had been quite a while since the last pig truck had passed, the advertised crab cakes, Virginia ham, hush puppies and apple fritters sounded good to us. When we arrived at the restaurant, we had second thoughts—but only for a minute—because it looked fancy. Not caring whether the other patrons liked the way we were dressed, we went in. Between courses, Lolly went out and got her maps. We sat around the table, oblivious to stares, looking at the maps and enjoying famous cooking at a famous spot.

"We're only about five miles from the Jamestown Ferry," Lolly pointed out, pushing the map my way for emphasis. "Do we have time to make a detour?"

I was well aware that we had detoured only once intentionally, that to Lincoln's birthplace, and once by mistake when I chose the wrong road and led us a mile down a beautifully landscaped lane leading to a county funny farm. This was no time to deny a ferry ride.

"Sure we do," I said, noticing some pressure slip away in the process and feeling good about it. I was the one with the reputation of holding us to the rigid schedule.

The ride down the side road, the fifteen-cent fare on the ferry, and the ride across the water on what was a gray, overcast day, seemed almost unreal. Then we sank into history again, staring almost in disbelief at the excavated foundations of the first church in Jamestown. We didn't even mind the commercial slant to what is actually a very fine glassblowing exhibit, depicting one of the earliest industries in the colony. The Park Service movie seemed better than most such productions. Then we were on the ferry, headed back to the Surry House for a refueling stop involving ice cream.

"Where are you from?" The man had just driven into the parking lot, and came right over to us.

We went through the usual explanation, but in a little more detail, because this person was obviously interested in bicycling and in us. We learned that he and his wife worked at one of the nuclear-related facilities in the area and had just purchased two new touring bikes.

"We're scheduled to make a ride along the West Coast from San Francisco to Los Angeles," he said. He looked at Lolly. "I know my wife would like to ask you a lot of questions. Will you be here a few minutes?"

"Yes," Lolly told him.

Shortly after he roared away, almost before we'd finished our ice cream, he was turning back into the parking lot, and this time he had his wife with him. She was an enthusiastic person, but you could tell she had some misgivings about their tour, which was only a month away. The next quarter hour went quickly as we responded to "What do you do about this?" and "What do you do about that?" It was obvious that the man was anxious to build his wife's confidence in their ability not only to make but to enjoy a bike trip. She was willing, but uncertain. Finally they got down to talking about bike seats.

"I don't know if you'll get accustomed to riding long hours on the seat or not," Lolly said. "I haven't. If we were riding only around six hours a day it would be fine. But after eight or nine hours, sitting just plain hurts."

Bill and I nodded agreement. We had somehow managed to avoid any serious saddle sores, but each of us experienced a lot of discomfort during the afternoon hours every day.

Lolly explained the importance of culverts and thick stands of trees and underbrush, and remembered to advise taking off one's helmet at such times. As the conversation came to an end—the questions were running out, and we had to go—it was gratifying to watch these two people gradually gather the fortitude to go ahead and make their ride, to answer the challenge. They were fifteen years our junior, and the effect

132 of our meeting had been interesting. The wife had begun with a tenta-

of our meeting had been interesting. The wife had begun with a tentative attitude towards the trip, but as Lolly supplied some of the answers
and helped put concerns to rest, we had seen her anticipation grow.

Suddenly I was reminded of the older fellow we met in the cafe in
Montana, who had snapped our picture from the pickup window to
show his wife in hope of convincing her that she, too, could go touring. I
don't know whether he persuaded her, but here with the couple in Surry,
we had been able to help and inspire. The man obviously felt more
justified, and his wife much more enthusiastic, towards their coming
bike trip.

Lolly and I looked at each other. Hadn't the possibility of inspiring
and helping someone been one of our justifications for the trip?

The afternoon was punctuated by more pig trucks, and just before
dark we rode into Smithfield. The obvious destination of the trucks was
a huge processing plant, specializing in ham. Its presence seemed to
indicate that we wouldn't be greeted by more trucks tomorrow. We set
out to find a motel.

There were no motels in Smithfield. The single bed-and-breakfast inn
was full, and wouldn't consider my suggestions that we would be
happy to rent a corner of its garage or storeroom. A check of the map
revealed no places to camp in the area, and after looking at the town, we
realized we needed help in finding a place to stay. We found a restaurant, ordered, and then I went to phone the local police.

"There are no campgrounds here," the voice over the phone told me.
"And be sure you don't camp in this area. It's not safe."

It was not long before dark, and when our dinner came, we ate
hurriedly. For some reason, we hadn't felt secure in the town when we
rode in, and the cryptic advice from the police hadn't put us at ease.

"I'm going to call the police again," I said. "Surely they know of some
place we can stay."

They didn't. In fact, I got the impression that they definitely didn't
care where we stayed as long as it was somewhere out of their jurisdic-
tion. Before going back to the table where Lolly and Bill were waiting, I
turned to the phone book and looked up the local churches in the yellow
pages. Of the first half dozen I called, every phone but one rang
unanswered. The lone response came from a machine asking me to be
sure to leave my name and number.

We were looking pretty glum as we finished dinner.

"Well, we can always ride down to the police station and say here we
are," I said. "We could sleep there, or in their jail."

"Might not be alone there," Bill said.

While Lolly paid for the meal, I went to the phone to try the rest of the churches. At the very last number left to try, a real, live person answered.

"What is it?" Lolly asked when I returned to the table. "You've got something, haven't you?"

My relief must have been showing more then I realized. "I talked with Richard Austin at St. Luke's, and he offered to let us camp on the grounds."

"Where's that?" Lolly asked.

"I don't know for sure, but we have some directions to follow. He said it's a few miles down the road."

It was too dark to see holes in the pavement when we rode into St. Luke's, but not so dark that the fine residence with its attached gift shop and entrance, guarding the park-like grounds beyond, didn't look like a real haven to us. We leaned the bikes against a post, and I knocked on the door.

"I'm Richard Austin." He was a large man, emanating a calm feeling of helpfulness, and you got the idea he enjoyed it.

I introduced the three of us, and after looking us over quickly, Richard made another offer. "I think it's going to storm tonight," he said. "If you don't mind, you can stay in the gift shop instead of camping on the grounds. Do you have sleeping bags?"

"Yes," Lolly answered. "That's great."

"Usually, " Richard said, "you could share my residence, but I have guests right now."

Bill said, "The gift shop is swell."

And it was, even when not compared with our previous prospects.

"Restroom facilities are right there," Richard said, pointing. "I'll just move this table, and there'll be plenty of room here on the floor."

We brought our bikes inside, carefully, because the usual gift shop inventory was spread over shelves, displays and racks. The oriental rug on the floor offered thick padding.

Richard turned toward the door. "I'll bring in a TV if you want."

"No, thanks. We're too tired to watch," Lolly said.

"I'll see you in the morning, then. If you want anything, just knock on my door."

We looked at each other for a minute, feeling some of the same ridiculous incredulity as when we found ourselves inside the rented gymnasium in Leaburg, Oregon. This too was an unlikely spot, sleeping on a fine rug in the middle of a gift shop crammed with inventory.

"Sure beats the jail," Bill observed.

We looked through some literature about St. Luke's and learned that today it is mostly used as a shrine. One of the oldest Protestant churches in America, its origins date back to the 1630's. Richard Austin, as the resident curator, was responsible for overseeing public visits to the shrine, for scheduling its special events—and, we were glad, for dispensing help and comfort to others in a sensitive, feeling way. Three cyclists in need of a place to stay were very grateful for his willing assumption of this burden.

We were up early in the morning, careful not to disturb those in the residence. We rolled up the bags, packed our panniers, and were about to leave when we saw Richard out working in the yard.

"Let me give you a tour," he said.

The original brick exterior of the old church seemed to radiate its history as Richard related it. As he explained the church's design characteristics, we could visualize its age. We marvelled at the span of centuries that have left St. Luke's in the hands of good people like Richard Austin.

Much of the ride down Highways 125, 337, 13 and 60 was in high-speed, metro traffic, with no possible escape from the travel lane. As the traffic became more hectic, many drivers honked at us or swerved towards us menacingly. We felt great stress. On this June 28, the fifty-sixth day of our ride, we had more than 50 miles to go to reach Virginia Beach.

Usually, we would have been able to talk about how near our goal was, and laugh about some of the things we had seen as we rode along. But under these conditions, we were white-knuckled and tight-jawed. There was no need for Lolly to watch for cars behind. I took the rear position, and tried to gain the extra few inches of roadway we needed to be able to ride at all. Traffic overtaking from the rear was steady, aggressive and fast.

And so the last miles of the ride were not enjoyable and carefree, as we would have liked them to be. We were forced to retreat into individual shells of concentration and determination to be able to ride at all through the city areas. At least the route was not uphill, but we had to shout between the passage of cars in order to communicate at all.

A couple of days before, we had confirmed our plan to stay over with Sherm, a cousin who lived in the Norfolk area. His help would make getting to the airport to fly back home much easier. Now, because the bridges leading to the airport don't allow bicycling, we were doubly glad that Sherm was going to meet us at the end of the ride.

Suffolk traffic, Portsmouth traffic, Norfolk traffic—each had its shot at us, and for several hours we seemed to be in the midst of one continuous close call. We had to take a rest alongside the busy thoroughfare, slopping down on a patch of grass beside the curb.

In spite of the vehicles speeding by, the "ENTERING VIRGINIA BEACH" sign made us grin at each other like kids. We would make it now, if we were able to stay alive in the traffic for another few miles. We took pictures of the sign and laughed, waiting for the tension of the ride to wear off so we would feel more like ourselves.

To get on the bikes again and face that bucking, rubber-tired, exhaust-spewing horde, each vying to see who could offend the most, was hard. For a few yards we wobbled tentatively under the traffic's impact. Then the discipline developed by 4,000 miles took over, producing the rail-straight style necessary when there was no room to bluff for. We headed towards the beach. Lolly spotted a sign that proclaimed a bike route down a side street, and we turned thankfully onto it and out of the pack.

It was just a short way to the beach now. Mild, short waves from the Atlantic washed in nervous little bursts up onto sand that marked the eastern edge of the country. Lolly was grinning; she had spotted the ocean first from a causeway crossing a small estuary arm. It seemed impossible that this was it, that we had ridden 4,150 miles across America. But here we were. Free of the heavy traffic, we began to relax a little as we sought a way down to the beach. We talked too loudly, and felt a detached wonder at our own reactions.

Lolly and I looked at each other, and we were beaming. I could see that she was happy, extremely happy. Did it matter right now if we had accomplished any of our other goals? We were here, we had made it. But for a minute I thought of Lynn Finnegan and her three companions, still riding westward as best we knew. Did our meeting help them in any way to stick with it, to keep riding even though the bike seat seemed sure to split you in half? And if our encouragement had helped, would seeing their trip accomplished cause them to be more confident in the rest of their lives?

What of Kevin Braun, the westbound cyclist we had met way back in Kansas—had he made it to his goal? Certainly sturdy Kevin would complete his ride. We hadn't missed his glances at us as we talked, measuring the gray in our hair and the trim of our bodies. Unquestionably he had been telling himself that if we could do it, so could he.

For some reason the cookies that our daughter Cindy had baked and sent flashed into my mind. That provender had been her way of encouraging us, and of being a part of the ride. Cindy's days of All-American women's volleyball play were fresh enough in her mind to make her respond with us to our challenge.

And then Lolly found a stairway between buildings that led down to the beach. We bumped the bikes slowly down the steps, and out onto the bright, reflective sand. A few bathers looked at us curiously, and a passing jogger said something uncomplimentary as he had to swerve to go around us. The sand was soft, and the narrow bike tires sank in deeply. The wet sand was firmer down by the water, and the bikes wheeled more easily. Then we were at the edge of the surf.

It was a moment of high emotion. This was the way the trip had started, with wheels in a different ocean and the bikes pointed the opposite direction. But here we were. I fumbled with the camera.

A competent-looking sunbather got up and took the camera from me.

"Let me," he said, focusing with a practiced flair and clicking off a few shots with each of our cameras.

"Thanks," I said. "We just rode across the country."

"I know." He grinned, and pointed at our jerseys. I had forgotten that we were wearing the slogan "Coast to Coast '86."

As we pushed the bikes back up the stairs and rode down towards The Strip, an electrical storm suddenly and magically emptied the beach of bathers. We rode along the bike path, but keeping to it didn't seem to matter now. A feeling of emptiness came flooding in to compete with the triumph of having completed the ride. We were through pedaling; we didn't have to push any more.

In making our airline reservations to fly home, we had been assured that boxes were available for the bikes. Now we could relax until Sherm came to pick us up. With luck we would see Bill's son Mark, who was coming down from Washington, D.C., to spend some time with us before we had to get on the plane.

I knew we would have a lot of work ahead when we got home. Already we had dates for slide shows about our ride. Connie had told Bill that TV and newspaper interviewers would be at the airport when we came in. I had a final column to write.

We went into a restaurant to eat while waiting for Sherm. I didn't care if anyone stared at us or not. Lolly and I touched hands and smiled. I knew she knew.

Our own ride of fifty-six days had been spawned so innocently: "Wouldn't it be fun to ride all the way across?" We were about to board a jet plane with hundreds of other people, to cross the continent in a mere five hours. Would any of our fellow air passengers ever know what it was like to cycle across America?

We hoped they would.

# APPENDIX

## 1

## Our Equipment

Here is our equipment list, complete for every item Lolly and I took along. Our bikes, panniers and a few important items are further discussed in this section. Bicycle tools are listed completely in Appendix 3. The items shown were selected for conditions of both heat and cold.

SELF-SUFFICIENCY FOR TWO

food for 2 days
2 light plastic cups
2 light plastic bowls
2 spoons
1 can opener
1 sharp folding knife
1 2-qt. aluminum pot & lid
1 Svea white gas stove
1 half-liter bottle of white gas & pour spout
6 match books
1 tube firestarter
1 tent
bicycle tools, parts, spares
2 sleeping bags
2 foam mattresses
1 lightweight air mattress
1 plastic ground cloth
various plastic bags for lining panniers, bike seat covers, etc.
2 flashlight/headlights with extra batteries
2 flashing taillights
first aid kit

PERSONAL CLOTHING:

3 pr. socks, wool
3 pr. underwear, polypropylene
1 long johns, top & bottom, polypropylene
1 lined jacket for cold
1 lined long pants for cold

1 set Gore-tex rain gear (jacket and pants)
1 pr. light wool gloves
1 pr. wind-shell gloves
waterproof shoe covers
2 pr. riding shorts
3 riding jerseys
helmet
padded riding gloves
1 balaklava
1 pr. riding/walking shoes
swimsuit
2 handkerchiefs

PERSONAL ITEMS:

2 1-liter water bottles
toothbrush & paste
razor
talcum powder
toilet paper
insect repellent
sunscreen lotion, lip balm
sun glasses
reading glasses
stick deodorant
dental floss
anti-chafe cream
soap and washrag
shampoo
comb
collapsible wash basin
small towel
camera & film
stamped envelopes
address, phone number list
wallet, ID, credit cards, cash
traveler's checks

MISC:

bungee cords
cable locks
maps (Bikecentennial's are excellent. We also bought road maps of
    each state along the way.)

LARGE EQUIPMENT ITEMS

Our bikes were Miyata One Thousand series. Bill built his bike on the One Thousand frame. Factory accessories were Shimano, with Biopace chain rings and strong cantilever brakes. Lolly liked the factory-supplied 700 x 32 chain tread radial tires for their apparently softer ride. I used Kevlar belted, center-ridged touring tires.

We changed the stems for the best fit. Bill's seat was the classic stretched leather, while ours were a top-of-the-line padded vinyl.

We changed the inner chain ring to a 26. That was a mistake on the conservative side, because paired with a 28-tooth cog on the cluster, the gearing was not low enough to enable us to spin on the steeper hills. I would recommend a lower gearing, as low as your derailleur will handle. The only time you are in that extreme gearing is when you need it, and then nothing else will do the job.

Panniers were of several brands; none excluded water. Plastic trash compactor bags, the heaviest you can buy, seem to stand up to chafing well and make excellent waterproof liners for panniers. Front racks were by Blackburn.

We kept all our valuable small items, things we didn't want to leave behind when we weren't with the bikes, in our left-front pannier. The bags made handy carrying cases, and we always had wallets, glasses, camera, etc., right at hand.

We each had 35mm cameras. I used my favorite Pentax, equipped with a short zoom lens. This combination allowed flexibility without requiring a lot of accessories. An auto-focus camera would have facilitated shots of moving riders.

The tent Lolly and I used was a free-standing, roomy model, which with fly weighs just over five pounds. Our sleeping bags are the five-pound, down-filled Kara Koram design by Eddie Bauer, very welcome on the cold first part of the trip but much too efficient later when it was warm.

CLOTHING

The wicking action provided by polypropylene in undergarments is effective. Most cycling shorts and jerseys are made of fabrics that have low absorbency factors also, and these are excellent in both hot and cold weather. We attempted to make dual use of major clothing items; for instance, our long johns were the second layer if the temperature was too low for basic shorts and jerseys. If it was really cold, we added our lined long pants and jackets, topped with Gore-tex suits. We often used Gore-tex right on top of the long johns. Gore-tex doubles very well for wind protection as well as rain gear.

Balaklavas are great face protection if you get caught in severe weather conditions. They can help prevent frostbite, reduce the effect of wind chill, and are invaluable when riding in snow, sleet or hail.

We chose to use combination riding/walking shoes because we knew we would be doing a lot of walking. This decision is another compromise, of course; regular riding shoes do a better job while riding.

Try to use a helmet at least as good as your head. Ours were by Bell. Nothing gives me shivers more than to see someone on a bicycle not wearing a helmet.

FOOD

You can eat in restaurants, cafes and diners if one is nearby and if you don't mind paying the bill. We carried food for two days at all times, because often there were no eating places where we found ourselves at the end of the day. In that case, we prepared a dinner and a breakfast at that spot. We tried to replenish our supplies before we camped again to avoid using up our reserve.

You can always buy something to eat within a few hours' ride. In any grocery you can find food to take along to prepare for meals. However, any substitutions in our reserve of food always meant additional weight and effort. We tried to carry the following items all the time:

> 2 freeze-dried dinners, heavy towards carbohydrates and protein
> 6 packets of instant oatmeal
> 8 granola-type trail bars (We found the best brands to be Granola, then Quaker Oats. We found the most energy in those containing the most nuts and grains, plus fruit, honey and carob.)
> 4 oz. dried fruit.
> 2 oz. Tang, the kind with sugar
> powdered chocolate, tea, cheese, peanuts for 2 days
> 2 bananas
> 2 oranges
> bread, peanut butter and jelly, or other lunch material for 2 days

The dinners and oatmeal are the basis of this system. Substitutions can be made for the snacks and lunches, but if you're going to carry dinners and breakfasts, it is hard to beat the first two items. Commercially available macaroni-and-cheese or other dinners can be used at less cost, but they will be far heavier and take more time, effort and fuel to prepare. We used Mountain House freeze-dried dinners, which required no cooking.

We also carried, and religiously used, a good multi-vitamin supplement.

# APPENDIX

## 2

## Conditioning and Training

You can't *train* if you're not in *condition*.

Condition, then, refers to the overall shape you're in, the condition of your body. Thanks to Lolly, good conditioning takes a high priority around our house. I try to stay in good shape through exercises, and maintain cardiovascular efficiency by taking brisk uphill hikes. We both ride bicycles for enjoyment.

When preparing for our ride across the country, we began to train for the specific abilities we felt were required. Generally this meant frequent riding at a pace that constantly challenged our condition. Gradually we began to cover more miles in the same length of time.

To become accustomed to all-day riding, we periodically took a ride of several hours. Not only did this tell us how we reacted to the need for sustained output, it also gave us experience with longer periods of sitting on the seat.

I firmly believe that few become completely acclimatized to long hours on the saddle. Long-distance racers must endure torture. But as we spent more hours on the saddle, our time of tolerable comfort did increase some. Never, however, did we reach the point where we were comfortable much longer than five or six hours.

Rollers or a wind trainer are great during bad weather. It is possible to achieve nearly all of the stresses of actual riding with the possible exception of duplicating climbing a steep hill with a loaded bike, which increases pedal pressure greatly. Our wind trainer got lots of use.

There is no point here in attempting to detail conditioning and training programs for touring or racing when this has been done so adequately in the following publications, and many others:

Borysewicz, Edward. *Bicycle Road Racing*. Brattleboro, Vermont: Velo-news, 1985.

Doughty, Tom. *The Complete Book of Long-Distance and Competitive Cycling*. New York: Simon and Schuster, 1983.

Ferguson, Gary. *Freewheeling: Bicycling the Open Road*. Seattle: The Mountaineers, 1984.

Kolin, Michael J. *Cycling for Sport*. Seattle: Velosport Press, 1984.

# APPENDIX

## 3

### Tools and Repairs

Since we anticipated riding together in a group, we could pool certain tools, which was a big weight savings. Here is what we took along for tools:

1 spoke wrench, checked for fit on all spokes
1 freewheel tool, checked for fit on all freewheel bodies
set of thin hub cone wrenches, checked for fit on all hubs
1 10mm combination wrench
1 small combination screwdriver, slot & Phillips head
1 chain rivet tool
1 8" adjustable (Crescent) wrench
1 5" Vise-grip pliers
1 tiny cutting/gripping pliers
1 set of metric Allen wrenches, sorted to fit all (but only all) Allen-head fasteners on all bikes
1 tire pump (per bike)
1 tire pressure gauge
1 set plastic tire tools (never used them)

OUR SPARE PARTS LIST

1 spare tire (per bike)
2 spare tubes (per bike)
1 tube patch kit, with extra cement tube and extra patches
8 extra front spokes
2 extra cables (long)
few chain links
$1/2$ oz. bearing grease
1 4-oz. squeeze bottle penetrating lubricant, with applicator tube
2 foot-square grease rags

This appendix is not intended to provide a course in bike mainte-nance, and it will be obvious to the experienced that there are repairs we could not accomplish, notably to the bottom bracket and headset, with the limited number of tools above. Modern, quality bicycles are quite trouble-free if maintained properly and not abused. Whether or not 60-pound panniers plus rider on a rough road constitute abuse, I'll leave up to you. However, here are the repairs and replacements we made during our trip:

> Bill broke two spokes the first three days, then bought a new 40-spoke rear wheel on the fourth day.
> Bill had to tighten a loose pedal spindle in Idaho.
> I had to tighten bottom-bracket bearings in Colorado, something we accomplished without the right tools. It was too late, however; the bearings were damaged, and bearings and spindle were replaced in a shop in Virginia.
> Bill, unable to achieve proper shifting, installed a new chain in Missouri. One day later, a shop installed a new rear cluster.
> Lolly had a rear-wheel trueing job in Illinois. All told, we had twelve flats, not bad for 25,000 wheel-miles. Three of those flats heralded the wearing out of the rear tires on each bike, somewhere around the 3,000-mile mark.

Bill did the bike maintenance, on an almost daily basis depending upon riding conditions. This usually amounted to an inspection, and lubing the chain and derailleurs very lightly. Bill adjusted the derailleurs every few days, before we encountered shifting problems, and consequently these systems performed almost flawlessly. When it comes right down to it, we probably could have ground along and finished the whole trip without any attention except to lubrication, and made it, with the exception of Bill's spoke problem and the initial trueing of Lolly's wheel after it went through a severe chuckhole.

By all means, if you're contemplating touring and don't speak wheel, take some instruction at your local bike shop so you will at least be able to make your wheel true enough to revolve, should it get bent.

Every two weeks or so, and after every rainy period, we de-gunked the chain, chain rings and cogs, and the derailleurs, and searched out any other part that was building up too much grime. Bikes are wonderful, though; they will not only take abuse, but they respond to care.

Among the excellent books on bicycle maintenance and repair are:

> Sloane, Eugene A. *Bicycle Maintenance Manual*. New York: Simon and Schuster, 1981.
> Glenn, Harold T. and Clarence W. Coles. *Glenn's Complete Bicycle Manual*. New York: Crown, 1973.

# APPENDIX

## 4
### Costs

The cost of a coast-to-coast tour could conceivably vary from less than the proverbial $5.00 a day to as much as you might want to spend, and would depend upon lodging, food choices and other activities. We fall somewhere in the middle, because we weren't trying to stay on a particular budget. We could have stayed in motels all the time (when they were available) or never, with a resulting difference in expense. Because of cost considerations, the three of us usually stayed in one room. On fifteen nights we camped at locations such as city parks, in the woods, or in church yards where no fee was required.

We chose mid-scale, family-type restaurants most of the time not only because the cost was moderate, but especially because the food was good and of a type we craved. Our home-nurtured habit of having steak or prime rib disappeared, and we became more interested in high-carbohydrate meals. Good salad bars were especially exciting to us. By choice we could have doubled our food costs, or lowered them some-what.

The following figures show what we actually spent on the trip. They do not represent any sort of recommended minimum or maximum expense.

| | | |
|---|---|---|
| Motel, lodging (35 nights) | $1061.39 | $30.33 per night average |
| Campgrounds (6 nights) | 44.00 | 7.33 per night average |
| Food (groceries and restaurants, 56 days) | 2103.81 | 12.52 per person/day |
| Airfare, Norfolk, VA, to Medford, OR (coach) | 864.00 | 288.00 per person |
| Shipping, boxes (3 bicycles) | 75.00 | |
| total | $4148.20 | $1382.73 per person |

TOURING EQUIPMENT

Since we already had all of our self-sufficiency gear from backpacking and other activities (sleeping bags, tent, stove, etc.), about all we had to purchase for touring was some means of carrying the gear. Panniers, the most common solution, represented an outlay of approximately $100 total for front and rear sets combined. Front racks, strictly a touring item upon which front panniers hang, cost $40 and up. We did buy helmet radios especially for the trip, but found them unreliable and unnecessary.

# APPENDIX

## 5

### Safety

The sport of bicycling can be safe and fun. It can be safest when you identify those factors that are likely to cause undesirable effects or injuries, and then avoid or minimize the causes. Causes fall into several categories, among which are:

    1. Motor vehicles and other moving objects
    2. Effect of heat, cold and exertion
    3. Road hazards

MOTOR VEHICLES

Unquestionably the most serious hazard faced by cyclists is being struck by a motor vehicle. I believe some precautions significantly lower the odds of such a catastrophe.

First, learn to be aware of traffic around you. Keep an eye on approaching autos, best done with a good rearview mirror. Sometimes the driver of an auto will not consciously see a cyclist, and this can have severe consequences. If you are watching the auto, you can often increase the clearance. The first rule in riding safely where traffic exists is to be able to see that traffic and be aware of what is going on.

Automobile drivers are becoming increasingly aware of cyclists; in fact, many drivers are cyclists also, but don't count on this. Remember that a bicycle travels slowly on the open road, and consequently may impact hundreds of drivers in the space of a few miles.

Ride straight without excessive weaving, thereby letting the driver know you aren't planning any abrupt course changes. Don't practice the wobbling technique we used on our ride; this was reserved for truly drastic conditions.

Ride on the shoulder if it is paved and smooth enough to do so. This increases the distance between you and each car that passes; extra distance means extra safety. It also shows the driver you are making an effort to minimize the conflict between the highway speeds of autos and the slower pace of bikes. Touring and recreational riders are safest riding single file unless it is possible to ride two or more abreast without being in the traffic lane. Single file makes conversation difficult, but you'll stay alive.

Increasing your visibility will give approaching drivers a better chance of seeing you. One effective gadget is a waving, fluorescent orange flag on a wand, either horizontal or vertical from the bike. If wind resistance of a flag sounds bad to you, then make sure that your clothing is highly visible. On our ride we wore the brightest yellow jerseys we could find. Other good colors are fluorescent chartreuse, or orange. The heck with color coordination; when you're on the road the object is to be seen. White helmets are far superior to black in visibility.

MOVING OBJECTS

Besides motor vehicles, moving objects hazards can include dogs or other animals; even chickens! I know a rider who had a very serious encounter with a deer that jumped out of the roadside brush and landed right across his chest. Develop an awareness for what is going on around you; use your eyes and ears, as well as your other senses.

COLD, HEAT AND EXERTION

Cold presents a hazard in several ways. Not only can it create glare ice on the road in shady spots, reducing your grip on the planet; it can reduce the slowing effect of your brake pads against your wheel rims. Cold can numb your hands and feet, blur your eyesight, and make you a less capable rider quickly. It can reduce joint flexibility and be a factor in knee injuries, or cause hypothermia, so beware. Protect yourself with adequate covering and insulation, or slow down, or both.

Sunburn, heatstroke and sunstroke are products of heat and exertion. Know the symptoms so you can treat each affliction correctly. Take courses in first aid. Remember that extreme heat affects tires and brakes.

Dehydration can occur regardless of temperature, so form the habit of drinking water at frequent intervals whether you are thirsty or not. If you become thirsty before you drink, you may already be partially dehydrated.

Remember that exertion increases your susceptibility to accident and to heat-related problems. You make better judgments and decisions when you are not tired.

ROAD HAZARDS

Safe riders keep a constant lookout for debris in their path. It is much easier on you, and your bike, to miss things like rocks, pieces of wood, metal and rubber on the pavement, and cracks, grooves and chuckholes in the pavement.

A word about riding at night: *Don't*. Road hazards are practically invisible, and so are you.

# APPENDIX
# 6
## Miscellaneous Statistics

MILES PER DAY

| Date | Day | Riding Mileage | Cumulative Mileage | Landmarks |
|------|-----|----------------|--------------------|-----------|
| May 4 | 1 | 80.6 | 80.6 | |
| 5 | 2 | 67.6 | 148.2 | |
| 6 | 3 | 85.2 | 233.4 | |
| 7 | 4 | 71.9 | 305.3 | |
| 8 | 5 | 85.2 | 390.5 | |
| 9 | 6 | 70.7 | 461.2 | |
| 10 | 7 | 75.1 | 536.3 | |
| 11 | 8 | 58.1 | 594.4 | Idaho border |
| 12 | 9 | 82.0 | 676.4 | |
| 13 | 10 | 52.1 | 728.5 | |
| 14 | 11 | 81.6 | 810.1 | |
| 15 | 12 | 88.9 | 899.0 | Montana border |
| 16 | 13 | 68.0 | 967.0 | |
| 17 | 14 | 67.2 | 1034.2 | Continental Divide |
| 18 | 15 | 69.2 | 1103.4 | |
| 19 | 16 | 73.8 | 1177.2 | |
| 20 | 17 | 73.0 | 1250.2 | |
| 21 | 18 | 69.0 | 1319.2 | Idaho border again |
| 22 | 19 | 29.9 | 1349.1 | |
| 23 | 20 | 66.9 | 1416.0 | Wyoming border |
| 24 | 21 | 104.5 | 1520.5 | |
| 25 | 22 | 76.5 | 1597.0 | Continental Divide (twice) |
| 26 | 23 | 76.7 | 1673.7 | |
| 27 | 24 | 63.7 | 1737.4 | |
| 28 | 25 | 60.2 | 1797.6 | |
| 29 | 26 | 100.0 | 1897.6 | Colorado border |
| 30 | 27 | 102.9 | 2000.5 | |
| 31 | 28 | 86.8 | 2087.3 | |
| June 1 | 29 | 58.3 | 2145.6 | Kansas border |
| 2 | 30 | 73.1 | 2218.7 | |
| 3 | 31 | 96.3 | 2315.0 | |
| 4 | 32 | 73.1 | 2388.1 | |
| 5 | 33 | 76.5 | 2464.6 | |

| Date | Day | Riding Mileage | Cumulative Mileage | Landmarks |
|------|-----|----------------|--------------------|-----------|
| 6    | 34  | 100.1          | 2564.7             |           |
| 7    | 35  | 68.8           | 2633.5             |           |
| 8    | 36  | 72.6           | 2706.1             | Missouri border |
| 9    | 37  | 77.0           | 2783.1             |           |
| 10   | 38  | 84.5           | 2867.6             |           |
| 11   | 39  | 58.9           | 2926.5             |           |
| 12   | 40  | 81.5           | 3008.0             | Illinois border, Mississippi River |
| 13   | 41  | 85.9           | 3093.9             |           |
| 14   | 42  | 70.7           | 3164.6             | Kentucky border, Ohio River |
| 15   | 43  | 86.6           | 3251.2             |           |
| 16   | 44  | 79.3           | 3330.5             |           |
| 17   | 45  | 61.5           | 3392.0             |           |
| 18   | 46  | 60.9           | 3452.9             |           |
| 19   | 47  | 69.2           | 3522.1             |           |
| 20   | 48  | 65.3           | 3587.4             | Virginia border |
| 21   | 49  | 49.4           | 3636.8             |           |
| 22   | 50  | 80.0           | 3716.8             | West Virginia, Virginia (again) |
| 23   | 51  | 85.5           | 3802.3             |           |
| 24   | 52  | 77.8           | 3880.1             |           |
| 25   | 53  | 61.1           | 3941.2             |           |
| 26   | 54  | 70.9           | 4012.1             |           |
| 27   | 55  | 78.5           | 4090.6             |           |
| 28   | 56  | 55.8           | 4146.4             |           |

Average mileage per day = 74.04

WEIGHT

Gear: as itemized in Appendices 1 and 3 above, stowed in front and rear panniers, plus sleeping bags, tent, pads and spare tire on rear rack; includes a half-liter of white gas (for stove) for both Bill and Don, but not the 2 liters of drinking water (about 4 lbs. additional) per bike. Each bike alone, unloaded but in touring configuration, weighed about 25 lbs.

|                          | Bill     | Don      | Lolly    |
|--------------------------|----------|----------|----------|
| starting gear weight     | 55 lbs.  | 55 lbs.  | 40 lbs.  |
| ending gear weight*      | 45 lbs.  | 45 lbs.  | 30 lbs.  |
| starting body weight     | 172 lbs  | 163 lbs  | 130 lbs. |
| ending body weight       | 160 lbs  | 155 lbs. | 122 lbs. |
| starting weight-on-tires | 256 lbs  | 247 lbs. | 199 lbs. |

*We estimate that the gear sent home reduced the weight in the panniers by about 10 lbs. per bike by the time we reached warm-weather configuration toward the end of the trip. At Virginia Beach, the starting weight-on-tires would be further reduced by our individual body loss.

An item we needed but were never able to find: for Bill, a standard bar of Ivory soap that would fit his soap container.

* * * * * *

Around our house are a lot of positive sayings that Lolly has collected from various sources and placed where they can't be missed: on mirrors, the bathroom wall, under the glass on my desk. Though the sayings vary, the common themes that affect attitude don't:

> *"Believe you can, and you will."*
> *"Be positive OF yourself and TO others, and you will get positive results."*

Can you imagine a bike racer who sprints ahead at the finish doing so because he is unsure of himself? If you want to go touring or to race, you must be motivated or you won't do it at all. If your motivation is strong enough, you will do it and probably have enough discipline to condition and train yourself to do it well. If your motivation is burning, all-compelling, you will have the discipline to excel. That same discipline will help you discover the strengths that are derived from a good mental attitude. And it is from this plateau that winners come.

May all your winds be favorable!